A Gathering of Words

I'VE BEEN THINKIN'

TERRY BECK

A Gathering of Words – I've Been Thinkin'

Copyright © 2015 by Terry Beck

All rights reserved. No part of this publication may be reproduced, distributed, or transmitted in any form or by any means, including photocopying, recording, or other electronic or mechanical methods, without the prior written permission of the publisher, except in the case of brief quotations embodied in critical reviews and certain other noncommercial uses permitted by copyright law. For permission requests, write to the publisher's representative at the address below.

Terry Beck
terry-beck@att.net

Ordering Information:
Quantity sales. Special discounts are available on quantity purchases by corporations, associations, and others. For details, contact the publisher at the address above.

Printed in the United States of America

TO RUTH DOSS...THANK YOU

*(To my loving wife Amber:
Ruth Doss was my high school English teacher)*

Table of Contents

Foreword i
Preface iii
I've Been Thinkin' 1
The Day I Walked Away From 1967 3
It Was Funny for a Minute 7
Slow? 11
Are You Friended? 13
The Redneck Justice League of Central Texas 15
LOL 19
Paper Doll Resurrection 21
It Thundered Louder Back Then 23
Don't Let Me Be The Reason 25
Nothing's Where It's S'posed to Be 27
I Blame the Road 31
The Strength of Silence 33
The Rock 41
Amber Goes Fishing 45
Simply Friends 49
Part of Me is You 51
The Night Everything Changed 53
I'm Not That Kind of Guy 55
It's a Beautiful Day in the Neighborhood 57
Stage 1 Water Restrictions - Burleson, Texas 59
Only Gonna Tell This Story Once 61
Revenge of the Mailbox 75
That Old Man on the Corner 77
Mom 79
A Good Day, Goats and All 81

Diary of a Project 85

Just One "Day" for Mothers? 89

If I Could Go Back 91

He Doesn't Dance Anymore 93

Whatever I Want 97

Still Alive & Kickin' 99

Our Hall Tree 101

The Back Porch 103

Transitions 107

'Splain Somethin' To Me 109

No Good Deed Goes Unpunished 111

Hey Mom, Hey Pop - It's Me 115

To Run and Play Again 117

Me and the Rifleman 119

Don't Know How We Did It 121

In a Heartbeat 123

We All Drank the Brownwood Water and Didn't Turn Out So Bad 127

Just a Simple Night 129

I've Been Thinkin'

FOREWORD

Following Terry Beck's thinking is a bit like rambling alongside a meandering stream that occasionally widens into a tumultuous river before receding into calm. Whether your excursion is relaxing, intriguing, amusing or thought-provoking, you'll find yourself noticing the previously unnoticed, perhaps for the first time.

Terry's retirement from railroading gave him time to corral his wandering thoughts into word pictures, sometimes whimsical, sometimes profound, and always resonant with the heart of a person who absorbs his surroundings and then reflects them back to the rest of us. We see what he sees and feel what he feels as he describes what passes for "normal" to most people. Looking at the world through his eyes and heart brings the realization that "normal" is precious, and never to be overlooked on the road to contentment.

Life is so very daily, and certainly filled with enough to keep a guy like Terry busy thinking for many years to come. I'm grateful he was considerate enough to retire so we can enjoy his gathering those thoughts into words that nourish and refresh the rest of us!

Mary Beth Smith
Dallas, Texas
2015

I've Been Thinkin'

PREFACE

Welcome to the second book in my series A *Gathering of Words*. I truly appreciate those who read the first book, *A Train Of Thought*, and hope you will find *I've Been Thinkin'* as entertaining. The first book was written to share my forty years of railroading. However, railroaders, bankers, lawyers, teachers and people of all occupations were once children with families and friends who affected their lives, and that is what this book is about.

Coming from a small town like Brownwood, Texas, I was fortunate to have been raised in an environment which allowed us to be close to a large percentage of its population and at least be familiar with the rest. In this book of short stories and essays, I will share my love and thoughts about family, friends, and living the simpler life.

Although we all live our own lives and have our own beliefs as well as memories, we have more in common than we sometimes realize. There is nothing that makes me feel better than for someone to say my stories take them back to memories of their own family and friends. Also, for someone to say, after reading some of my thoughts, they have often felt the same way but have never put it into words, gives me a special feeling.

I want to thank all my wonderful family and trusting friends, as well as all the others who have given me the support I've needed to do something I never felt I would be able to do. Thank you to all who provided me with the subject matter. (You will know who you are!) Finally, I want to again thank publisher Mary Beth Smith of Park Cities Publishing and her staff for their hard work and support. There are too many to personally thank for making this book a possibility, so thank you all!

Family and Friends Always!

Terry Beck
Mills County, Texas
2015

A Gathering of Words

I'Ve Been Thinkin'

I'VE BEEN THINKIN'

I've been thinking, more or less, for a long time. First there was "suggestive inducement thinking." This is where Mom and Pop would point at an object and repeat its name or title over and over and over, until I would finally repeat the word in order to get them to move on to something else. Hopefully, that something else was lunch.

Then, along came "mandatory thinking". This was encountered in the school years where you were required to train in the ability to think, and as a result, actually learn. Then, you where tested and graded on your ability to think, with the results displayed every six weeks for all to see.

Next up was artificially, or "chemically induced" thinking. I really don't think the learning process was involved in this particular era. It seems that this time frame, although rather vague, was filled with, what I felt at the time, extremely imaginative thoughts that were rarely ever transformed into any actual action. I can recall thinking at the time, "Wow, this is really far out. It just doesn't get any cooler than this." Fortunately for me, I managed to pass through this thinking phase relatively undamaged. Now that I think back, I probably didn't really have as much fun as I thought I did.

Finally, I arrived at the "thinking for profit" stage, or labor related thinking. I entered the work force, where I was required to think for pay. I quickly learned that the more I thought and the better my thoughts, the more money my employer was willing to pay me. This phase of the thinking process worked out pretty well for me nearly forty years. Then I got tired of thinking for money. It was becoming obvious that my particular thinking process was becoming obsolete and that my thinking did not involve those I loved as much as it should have. I decided that I was no longer going to think for pay. I retired.

I didn't quit thinking; I just ceased to think for the above mentioned reasons. Now I think just for the heck of it, and I catch myself thinking all the time. I have so much to think about. Some of it is real, some of it is wishful, but all of it is worthwhile. I take journeys back into the past, the joys and the heart breaks, the mistakes and the successes, the family and the friends. I find that my mind and my thinking process are a valuable part of what I am now. I am no longer graded on my thinking abilities. I no longer let chemicals or other artificial products tilt my thinking toward the unreal or unreachable. I no longer think for pay. I think because it is a beautiful place to be. Whether it is experience based, imagination based or a search for a better way, thinking is so easy now.

I realize that there will be challenges both physically and mentally, now and in the future, but currently the world of thought is bright and has endless possibilities. There are so many who have provided the fuel for my dream-filled thought processes. For all who have contributed, I say "Thank you, and I'll be thinking about you"!

I've Been Thinkin'

THE DAY I WALKED AWAY FROM 1967

Everything that happened to me from birth through high school occurred for a reason, mostly with the guidance and urgings of my parents, teachers, relatives and other older folks. I learned the things you are supposed to learn. I learned to love, share, play, work, grieve and pray. I went through the normal trends of friendship from childhood playmates to schoolmates, from teammates to running mates. There were relationships made up of family, close friends, casual friends, acquaintances and those who, even though I knew their name, I didn't really know.

There is much that I remember from those days. It's really funny that a lot of the things I remember best are some of the more trivial things, things that make me laugh, things that make me feel warm inside, things that make me feel a little sad because they are so far gone. I can remember sitting by the radio nightly, doing my homework while listening to DJ Riney Jordan, and waiting for a dedication that involved someone I knew and occasionally getting up the guts to call in a dedication myself. Of course the next day I would deny that it was me that called it in when approached by friends that had heard it the night before.

I remember Teen Timers held at the old Community Center. I loved Teen Timers and could hardly wait from week to week in anticipation of going. I really don't know why I loved it so. I was scared to death of asking a girl to dance, even though Mom had done a pretty good job of teaching me to dance. I would live for the "Lady's Choice" announcement and hope that a girl would ask me to dance and that it would be a slow song -- "Blue Velvet" would be fine.

There are other things I remember: my first car (1956 Nash Ambassador), tight white Levi jeans, Cross Trainer running shoes (black with white stripes on the side) and butch haircuts. I can remember making the drag to see who was out and about, sitting at the "Maid" having one of the best chocolate milkshakes or malts in town and the orange plastic giraffe stuck on top of the shake. I don't know why a giraffe, but I bet I had a hundred of them hanging from the netting over the sun visors in my car. Mr. Cole and his son Peewee ran the Dairy Maid and even though Mr. Cole appeared to be an old grouch, we knew he loved us. Why else would he have put up with us as long as he did?

I can remember camping out with my buddies on the Country Club grounds, water skiing on Lake Brownwood in the summer and going to the Midnight Matinee with my friends, when my folks would let me. I can remember climbing to the top of the huge concrete water tower in Camp Bowie and hearing the old farmer out in his field yelling, "Get down from there, you crazy idiots!" Thinking back, I think I agree with the old farmer: we were idiots.

Then there was good ol' Brownwood High School itself. I can remember the smell of the grass as we attacked football practice after school. I recall the sounds of the band as they went through their practice rounds and the sight of the drill team going through their paces. I remember hearing the last school bell of the day and seeing my fellow students filing out of the building and toward the parking lot, some walking and visiting and some in a dead run. I can still hear the roar of some of the 'souped up' cars cranking in the parking lot and hearing them leave a little rubber as they made their departure.

There are so many things that I still remember about high school; the loud chatter of the lunchroom before the start of school and again at lunch, Miss Mac's choir class where we learned more than just music, the assemblies (the fun ones, and the not so fun ones), the bustle of the locker rooms between classes and the sound of books hitting the floor because someone had rigged someone else's locker, sitting in the classes with the glass wall facing the walkway outside and watching fellow students walking by during class and wondering why they were heading to the office, I can remember the library, but I don't know why – I really never used it that much. I can still hear the roar of the pep rallies. I can still remember the smell of cigarettes as you walked into the bathroom and a fellow student standing there with a halo of smoke over his head as he tried to look innocent. I was always amazed at how well and how fast they could hide a burning cigarette.

Some of my fondest memories involve Friday night football. The noise of the full stadium, the sounds of the band, the cheerleaders, the drill team and the fans all made this night magical. I remember the huge Mums that the girls wore. Some looked more like parade floats than a corsage, but the girls always looked extra pretty on Friday night. I fell in love with many a Brownwood girl, but most never knew it. Oh yeah, the Victory Dances - can't forget them! It seems like we had a bunch of those.

Then 1967 came around and the day I walked away from all these memories came as well. I wish I would have realized what I was leaving behind. I wish that I had known then how many special, talented, and intelligent people I had the good fortune of sharing my early life with. We all grew up in the same town, drank the same water, shopped at the same stores, prayed to our God and listened to the same radio stations. Those are some of the things that will forever make us connected.

My regrets are few. I regret that I had good friends that I thought would be close forever and we haven't been. I regret that there are those of my youth that I didn't get to know better, based on what I know of them now.

They say you can't go back, but I think you can. Taking a different road each trip, I make the journey back to 1967 on a regular basis. Each time I walk back, I realize it was only the beginning – not the end.

I have done some foolish things. Some I realized were foolish and did them anyway. Thankfully, although not always, I was the only person aware of my nonsensical actions or thoughts. With every brainless and occasionally idiotic act, although frivolous to most, I became a better person.

Fortunately, there is little left for me to learn the hard way.

I've Been Thinkin'

IT WAS FUNNY FOR A MINUTE

It was the summer of 1967 in Brownwood, Texas. I had just finished the first eighteen years of my development into what I am today. I was fortunate to land a summer job working for the Texas Highway Department as a lab technician at White Mines, or as most of us local folks knew it, the "Rock Crusher". I was hired to work for two months before going off to college.

The state had a small lab located on White Mines property for the express purpose of testing all outbound materials (rock, gravel and asphalt) to insure that it met all state required specifications. There were four or five state employees that alternated shifts at the lab, 24 hours a day. We worked closely with White Mines employees, and I became friends with many of them. I was fascinated by the everyday operation of the facility and the abilities of those that worked there. The huge machinery, the rock quarries and the small lakes used for washing the rock were an everyday venture for me.

When my duties would allow, I would watch the huge front-end loaders work. It amazed me how these men would operate these huge machines as if they were toys. These loaders were almost as large as the lab building in which I worked. I loved to watch them charge a pile of gravel with the huge bucket only inches off the ground, sliding under the pile and in what seemed like a synchronized dance move, swing around and drop the load in the back of a huge truck. It looked so easy and smooth that I became convinced that I could do it.

Then the day arrived. One of my favorite operators saw me standing and watching him work. He climbed down from the loader and asked me if I wanted to give it a try. He didn't have to ask twice. As I climbed up on the huge machine, the operator was giving me instructions on the do's and don'ts of operating the machine. I'm not sure I heard much of it. I began to move the machine slowly at first. It was as if I was driving a building. Then my confidence kicked in, or should I say my over-confidence kicked in. There was this gravel pile near the lab building that had been bothering me because it was in the parking area. I couldn't figure out why they had never moved it.

I decided that pile was going to be history. I squared the loader around and charged the pile with the bucket only a few inches above the ground. It became apparent rather suddenly why no one had moved the pile. You see, it wasn't a pile of gravel. It was a pile of concrete covered with a layer of dust and dirt. The machine came to an abrupt halt. I didn't. I was thrown up on top of the steering wheel and the knob on the steering wheel buried into my stomach knocking the breath out of me. It seems that one of the things that I didn't hear the operator tell me was to make sure I engaged the seat belts. The operator ran over to the machine and by the time he had climbed up to me, I had regained my ability to breathe. I assured him that I was fine. I did, however, bear the perfect imprint of the steering wheel knob right above my belly button for a couple of weeks.

There was always something going on around the lab. One day as I was walking out of the lab, a White Mines Foreman drove up and motioned for me to come over to his pickup. He had one of the stainless steel containers with a clear plastic lid that we used to hold lab samples on the front seat. He wanted me to see the small rattle snake that he had caught and placed in the container. After a short conversation he got out of his truck and asked if he could use the restroom facilities in our lab. After he went into the lab, I removed the container with the snake in it and hid it behind the building. In its place I placed an identical container on the seat laying on its side with the lid off laying next to it. Shortly the foreman came out of the lab and got into his truck while looking out the truck and talking to me.

He then placed the truck in gear, and as he waved good-bye, started driving down the hill slowly from the lab toward the front gate. I stood watching as he reached the halfway point down the hill. Suddenly his truck door flew open and the foreman bailed out of the still moving pickup. He began slapping his pant legs with his hands and pulling his shirt-tail out as his pickup continued its slow roll down the hill, coming to a stop as it nudged a gravel pile at the bottom of the hill. He then ran down the hill and slowly approached the truck. Before I could get down to him he had already begun the process of pulling the seats out of the truck. He removed the floor mats and practically stripped the inside of the vehicle.

Sometime while all this was going on I had determined that things had already gone too far and that it would be to my best interest not to tell him what I had done. What can I say? I was eighteen years old and if you had seen the look on his face, you wouldn't have told either.

For several weeks everybody was talking about the "snake episode". My fellow State employees just couldn't believe how funny it had been. That's when I made a mistake. I couldn't resist telling them what I had done. What I didn't take into consideration was that they had known this foreman a lot longer than they had known me. Several more weeks had passed and all seemed to be going well in my final days of work. Then one day one of my fellow employees hollered from outside the lab and told to come outside. I got up from the desk, put on my hard hat and headed for the door.

What I didn't know was that my old friend the foreman had used one of the huge front end loaders, dipped the bucket into one of the quarry lakes and scooped up several hundred gallons of water. He had positioned the machine back behind the lab, and had the bucket raised up and positioned directly over the front door.

As I walked out the door I noticed that there was an unusually large group of guys standing around some distance from the lab. As I walked out the door and cleared the building, the foreman completed his revenge with a simple manipulation of the bucket control.

That was forty-two years ago and to this day, I walk out of small buildings very slowly and carefully.

I learned a valuable lesson that day: a hard hat doesn't help much when you have three hundred gallons of water coming down on you.

There are those who make life changing decisions based on the suggestion of someone whose OPINION is nothing more than a belief that is a little stronger than an impression, but less firm than actual knowledge. Decisions should be based on fact, not opinions.

Of course, that is just my opinion.

SLOW?

The other day I heard someone say, "He's just a little slow", when making reference to someone's intelligence level. As a matter of fact, I may have uttered those words myself a time or two in the past. I know what is insinuated by the phrase, but for some reason, when I heard it this time it got me to thinking. Is it really all that bad to think a little slow? I'm not even sure how you would measure the speed of someone's thinking. What would be the advantage of a fast thinker over a slow thinker? I guess one thing would be that the fast thinker could show his rear before the slower thinker. Or, it might be that the slower thinker might realize the possibility of showing his rear as he slowly travels through the thinking process, and in doing so, is able to change his thinking direction in such a way that he does not show his rear at all.

I know that a fast walker is more likely to miss some of the scenery, or overlook a tripping hazard as they hurriedly traverse the pathway to their destination. The slower walker is better able to take in the sights and pick and choose where his next step might be. Then there is the slow talker. They are many times perceived as being on the low side of the intelligence scale, especially by the fast thinkers. When a fast thinker is listening to a slow talker, his mind is so far ahead of what the talker is saying that they reach a conclusion about what is being said before it is actually said, and by doing so, they actually have no idea what was said anyway. Probably the most dangerous combination is a slow thinker that is a fast talker. They are the ones that after getting a dozen or so words into their statement suddenly realize, "Crap! Where am I going with this mess? I wish to heck I'd just kept my mouth shut!".

Some of the brightest people I know are slow talkers. They think carefully, and probably slowly, and consider what they are going to say, if it is what needs to be said, and what effect it will have on the listener before they begin to speak. If you are a slow thinker, this is not a problem. However, if you are a fast thinker you will have to exercise patience to reap the benefit of what is being said. I have also had the pleasure of knowing some fast talking, fast thinking people who are also mentally gifted and have the ability to gear down to a more compatible speed to allow slower thinkers time to absorb what they have to offer.

As for me, I'm proud to be a slow thinker. There is one thing that should be made clear at this point: There are slow thinkers that are not very smart, just as there are fast thinkers that are not smart, but prove it faster. For the most part, I am also a slow talker, unless I get excited or mad. I have learned with age to use this slow thinking and slow talking to my advantage. When asked a question, I pause, tilt my head to the side, look up toward the heavens, stroke my goatee and then give my response slowly. For some reason, this makes whatever you say seem wise and meaningful, even if you say you really don't know the answer.

There are times when folks don't use their brain at all at any speed. They simply mimic what others have said or done, and follow the more popular crowd. It saves them from all the pain that can result from serious thought. There are times that I don't feel like thinking, so I wait for someone else to do it for me. However, it is usually one of those fast thinkers and I end up having to rethink it slowly and then make my own decision. For some of us, thinking is a challenge at any speed. If I do a lot of thinking, it makes me tired. If I try to think fast, it gives me a headache.

Despite being a slow talking, slow thinking type guy, I think I am rather intelligent. I just proved that by using the word 'rather' in the preceding sentence.

I've Been Thinkin'

ARE YOU FRIENDED?

It would appear it is somewhat easier to make friends than it used to be. It seems almost everything about friends is easier, making them, keeping them, and getting rid of them. We can visit them without getting out in the weather, if it's too hot, too cold or even if it's just right. We don't have to worry about what to wear. If we aren't in the mood, we don't even have to brush our teeth if we decide to visit. The really neat thing, especially if you haven't seen the friend in a long time (or ever), you can post whatever year photograph you desire or none at all. With this new friend system, I probably have more verified friends than I have ever had before. What is really neat, I have a list, and on this list I can actually categorize my friends, and even limit how much contact they have with me. Some folks actually have more friends now than the total number of people that lived in their hometown.

On the other hand, I have made new friends and gotten back in touch with some old friends and have learned more about them now than I ever knew before. It even upsets me some, because I have wasted so much time in getting back in touch with people I've known in the past. I'm sure one thing that makes these new or rekindled friendships so much better is that I'm so much smarter than I used to be. Matter of fact, I have noticed most of my friends are smarter than I remember them being before. It's harder to be lonely now with all these friends just a click away. You can chat even if you really don't have anything to say. Sometimes you don't even have to visit. You just turn on your magic box, or tablet, or phone just to check and see who else is up at that time of night and then smile, log off and feel a little better about things than you did before you logged in.

So, there's making and keeping friends the old fashioned way, and there's this new fangled way. I like them both, and hope that both are here to stay, even if we do have to learn a new modification to this modern way every couple of weeks or so.

At the risk of making some of my younger friends a little uncomfortable, I think I'm going to lean a little more toward the old fashioned way of making and maintaining friends. There is just something about touching, kissing, warm embraces, firm handshakes and being able to count the wrinkles of wisdom etched in the face of a touchable friend.

Either way - Old School or New - Consider yourself 'friended'!

I've Been Thinkin'

THE REDNECK JUSTICE LEAGUE OF CENTRAL TEXAS

Let me begin by saying this story may or may not be true. If true, any similarity to any persons or places is purely coincidental. I will simply tell the story and you can determine any truth, value or substance worthy of retaining or passing on.

The year was somewhere between 1966 and 1968. The location was a small college about half way between Brownwood and Ft. Worth, Texas. The school year was well underway and the habits of those attending were pretty well established. Dorm life had formed its cliques and sub groups and, as with any dormitory, this dorm had formed a personality of its own. One particular group was made up of mostly freshmen from several Texas cities, some large, but mostly small. This group was not into fraternities or social clubs. They would study, eat and generally hang out together. Each one of this group came from a closely knit family and were making the necessary adjustments to survive in their first journey from home. They were forming a new type of family, a family of support and strength.

This dorm would have been a comfortable abode for this particular group had it not been for one person. This person was a fellow resident and student who delighted in making life for those around him miserable. He was a loud, obnoxious, self-centered jerk with a serious drinking problem. He apparently came from a family with money and used this campus more as a hangout than an institution of higher learning. There were other things about this guy that were noteworthy; he was huge and he was mean.

Every night he would go out, usually to Mingus, Texas, and drink with a couple of equally huge, tasteless guys. No one was sure what these other two guys did or where they came from. Almost every night they would come back to the dorm raising cane, hollering obscenities, playing loud music and slamming doors. They would turn over trash cans, knock on doors, and generally make a mess of things.

Everyone in the dorm, including the previously mentioned group of freshmen, were victimized by this thug at one time or another. However, there was one member of this group who seemed to bear the brunt of his attacks. Probably the most easygoing person of the group, he also worked as the janitor of the dorm in order to help pay for his education. He took great pride in his job and worked very hard keeping the dorm in the best shape possible. He was such a likable person that others in this group gladly helped with his chores from time to time if he needed study time or if they had an activity or interest coming up.

For no apparent reason, the dorm bully delighted in trashing the halls, bathrooms and other dorm facilities after the janitor had put in hours of work. He would come in at night and urinate in the halls and if he got sick from all the drinking, he thought nothing of vomiting on floors, walls or in trash cans. Yes, the bully was approached by many, turned in many times and on occasion was actually disciplined by the school. But, for whatever reason, the discipline was never serious and served as no deterrent to his angry habits. People became reluctant to take action because of the lack of apparent interest, and the retaliatory threats issued by the bully.

One cold, early December day a couple of the freshmen had an opportunity to go deer hunting, and late that afternoon managed to shoot a pretty nice buck. The deer was brought back by the dorm parking lot and was shown to the rest of the group, one of whom had access to a meat locker. This person accompanied the hunters to the meat plant and used his key to allow them to put the deer in cold storage until it could be processed the next day. It was when they got back to the dorm that a plan was born. A plan to dish back some misery to the dorm bully.

The bully, as expected, left his third floor room about 7 PM. The group knew that they would have until at least midnight before he would return. At 11 PM they went back to the meat locker and retrieved the deer. They were able to sneak the deer up to the third floor of the dorm.

The janitor reluctantly let them use his master key, and in just moments they had the deer in the bully's room. They turned back the covers on the lower bunk bed and covered the sheet with a large piece of plastic. They then laid the deer on the bed with its head resting on the pillow. They covered the deer with another piece of plastic and pulled the cover over it up to its neck. It really looked peaceful, or so I've been told. They turned out the light and left the room. There was nothing to do then but to wait for the return of the drunken bully.

As expected, a little after midnight, the dorm bully could be heard stomping and staggering up the stairs. He staggered down the hall singing loudly all the way to his room. He went into his room and could be heard throwing his boots and clothes around the room. Then the click of the light switch could be heard and his lights were out. There was silence for about fifteen more seconds. Then came a blood curdling scream. It was really amazing how high pitched this scream was coming from such a bear of a man. His door swung open and he ran screaming down the hall in his underwear.

As soon as he was out of sight, the justice squad ran into the room, grabbed the deer and plastic, and within just a few minutes had the evidence gone and on the way back to the meat locker. About ten minutes later, the bully could be heard coming back down the hall accompanied by the Dorm Supervisor and the Campus Security Officer. He was raving on and on about the huge animal or demon that had come within an inch of taking his life. After they were in the room for a few minutes, the screaming finally stopped. It was determined that Mr. Bully would be better served not to stay in the dorm that night and he was escorted from the building.

The next day, there were several non-students moving all the personal belongings out of the bully's room and his car was towed from the parking lot. He was never seen again. The talk was that his parents had finally tired of his antics and had committed him into a treatment facility. The dorm became a pleasant place to live. It was as though the cloud that had hovered over the building had been blown away and there was nothing but sunshine and laughter left behind.

You might wonder if anyone ever confessed about the happenings that December night. NO. You might also wonder if there was any guilt shared by the group. As a group, NO. However, there was one member of the group that worried about the results of that night, and had a problem letting it go. It was the person abused the most who was the most forgiving: The janitor, a heck of a man and friend.

By the way, the deer provided some of the best jalapeno cheese summer sausage you could ever want.

Or so I've been told…

LOL

When you're sitting by yourself, and you see or think of something funny, do you laugh? If so, do you laugh out loud, do you just smile, or do you just think "Man that was funny"? If something humorous happens and there is no one there to see it, is it still funny? Why is something funny to one person and possibly offensive to another? Does the mood you are in determine how funny something is, or does your mood just affect the way you respond to humor? Is a sense of humor really a sense, or is it simply a reaction to something that our true senses conceived?

I think laughing makes you feel better, but you don't have to feel good to laugh. I think laughter can be contagious. You can walk up to someone who is laughing hysterically and begin to laugh yourself before you know what is so funny. Is laughing out loud simply a means of letting those around you know that you think something is funny, or is laughing a physical response to a mental process?

The answer to most of these questions is "I don't know". I do know that laughter makes me feel better. I know that other people who laugh make me feel better. I appreciate those who have a sense of humor and don't mind sharing it. I realize that not everything is always happy and with most of my emotions, I do not hold back. I have a tendency of showing my emotions freely. If crying is called for, I will cry. If I get mad, regretfully, I generally show my anger. If I love, it's usually not a secret. Along with love, happiness and laughter are my favorites.

I laugh a lot, and frequently LOL.

I've Been Thinkin'

PAPER DOLL RESURRECTION

In early 2003 I made a trip back to Brownwood to clean up and straighten out my Mom's old storage shed in her backyard. Dad had passed away the year before and Mom had no idea what was stored in the old shed. In the process of cleaning out the shed, I found an old dirty folder covered in spider webs, dust, dirt dobber nests, and water stains. I brought the old folder out of the shed to where Mom was sitting in a lawn chair, and asked her to look at it and determine if it was something to keep or something to trash. She slowly opened the folder and after peeking in said, "Oh my word, it's my old paper doll set from when I was just a little girl." She had to clear her throat and with a tear in her eye, she said, "I thought I had lost that years and years ago."

All the pieces to the doll set were stained and covered with dust and dirt and barely recognizable. I asked Mom what she wanted me to do with it. She just shook her head and said it was a shame that it was ruined, but it might as well be thrown away. I told her that before we did that, perhaps I might take the paper doll set to Amber and see if she could salvage anything at all. She agreed and I brought the set home to Amber.

Amber never saw the dirt and grime. All she could see was the potential for beauty and the memories of someone dear to me. Amber located someone she trusted and asked for assistance in restoring the doll set if possible. Most all the pieces were saved and Amber had the pieces you now see framed. On the back of the framed set Amber had them make a pouch in which the rest of the pieces are stored or be available if someone wanted to change the display at a later time.

I brought the finished product back to Mom and she was thrilled to no end, and amazed that the folder of dirty, dusty, aged paper could once again look so pretty. She passed the set on to Amber on that same day, saying she knew it was going to a loving woman who would care for it so others would know the joy that she had once had.

Now Mom is gone, too, but her childhood treasure still has a place in our home. Here it will remain, until it is once again passed to another generation as Mom looks down and smiles.

I've Been Thinkin'

IT THUNDERED LOUDER BACK THEN

I sat alone, but not without company, out by The Creek this afternoon. I had been working in what started out as a typically miserable hot Summer day in Texas. However, also typical with Texas weather, a heat spurred thunderstorm began to build in the west and, as I sat back in my favorite chair, I could feel a cooler breeze laced with the unmistakable smell of rain. Then the slow rumble of thunder began to build in the distance. I closed my eyes and laid my head back so that my face was pointing upward toward the canopy of Crepe Myrtle leaves swaying with the cool wind.

Then came a second rumble of thunder, this time heard by the ears of a young boy sitting in the safety of his home in Brownwood, Texas. It seems storms came more often, the thunder much louder and the winds blew with violent velocities. Yet, I don't remember any real fear. I can remember, as a crash of thunder shook the house accompanied by a blinding flash of nearby lightning, I would glance back toward Mom or Dad and if they appeared unconcerned, so was I. I would sit inside the front door with my face pressed against the glass window and watch nature's show. I don't know that I have felt that same sense of security since.

Another clap of thunder, this time closer and louder, and I open my eyes as I feel a tapping on my lower leg. I lean forward and there at my feet is Beaux Bo, looking up at me as if looking for an indication that all was well. I reach down and place him in my lap just as another barrage of thunder rumbles near and a fine mist begins to work its way through the thick leaves of the Crepe Myrtle trees. This time, Beaux Bo rares up with his front feet on my chest and licks my cheek nervously.

I give him a reassuring hug, pick up his ball and we walk slowly toward the house as I tell Beaux Bo, "Let's go in, get something to eat and watch it rain."

I've Been Thinkin'

DON'T LET ME BE THE REASON

There is always a certain amount of emotion involved when you observe someone crying. Even if it is a perfect stranger, certain emotions can be stirred; sympathy, sadness or even anger. Seeing someone else cry, especially a loved one, can be hurtful to an emotional observer. Even self-professed hardened observers are sometimes moved.

To see a face slowly melt from a happy carefree expression to one of heartbreak and sadness gives one's heart the heavy dreadful feeling of regret. Eyes, clear and trusting, slowly melt into a watery gaze of hurt. You wish things could be different. You wish you could have prevented the cause, or even change places with them. Yet, there will always be reasons and there will always be causes.

You chastise for the wrong they have done. You are the one who says no, when everyone else is getting to go. These things are done with the sternness and conviction necessary, all the while with a lump in your throat and a hurt in your heart. Wouldn't it be nice if the answer could always be yes?

You speak quickly in response to emotion, and you can tell by the hurt expression and the tearing eyes that you have spoiled the moment, all because of reactionary verbal abuse. You wish the words could be unsaid or be forgiven. However, the words can never be unsaid and who's to say if forgiveness comes, that it is complete?

There will always be sadness, and tears will fall. I pray that I will always be there for those who are in need, when their tears begin to fall and their hearts are heavy. I also pray, when fate will allow, don't let me be the reason.

The frenzy is over. The threats and accusations have ceased. My health is no longer threatened and the house has been put back in order. The appropriate apologies have been administered, so hopefully we can return to a normal life...I found the TV remote!

I've Been Thinkin'

NOTHING'S WHERE IT'S S'POSED TO BE

I had nothing but goodness in mind when all this started. Help out a fellow and his family in need and make Amber happy at the same time. It all seemed so simple, so good. I wouldn't have to do much of anything. It would happen very quickly, so there would be little inconvenience. It would only involve a couple of rooms, minimizing disruption of my routine, and I would have to do very little other than write a check. (Did I already say I wouldn't have to do anything?)

Things started out innocently enough just prior to the Christmas holidays when my neighbor, Jake, introduced me to a painter who was doing some work on his house for an unbelievably low price. The painter and his wife seemed sincere and very professional and after seeing their work and talking with them, I agreed to let them do some much needed painting/repair work on our house. They painted the outside trim, repaired some water damaged ceiling inside the house, and repaired and painted the walls and ceiling in the garage. I was very pleased with the quality of their work, and amazed at the low prices he charged. I paid them for their work and told them that was all I needed for now, but that I would keep them in mind if something else came up in the future. They were very appreciative, packed up their stuff and left, and that was that.

A few days later – that's when I had my brainstorm. I asked Amber how she would like to get our master bedroom and bath repainted. Amber reacted like I would have if someone asked me to go on a fishing or golfing trip for a week. So, with that, I called the painter and the plan was set. It was going to be so good, so easy (See first paragraph) and I was going to be the hero.

Then it began. The night before the painter was to arrive, Amber wanted to take all her pictures and knickknacks off the walls and move the smaller pieces of furniture into another room to help the painters a little. I agreed. However, after we began, I was told to dust every object I removed from the wall, as well as each piece of furniture prior to moving them to another room. Then we had to vacuum and clean all the doors and trim work, again to save the painters some time. Then we had to clean the bathroom, because we certainly wouldn't want strangers thinking we didn't keep a clean potty room. It was after midnight before we were ready to hit the sack.

The next day the painter and wife (Helper) arrived. They immediately stretched canvas sheets on the floor through the living room, hall and into our bedroom. They shoved all the remaining furniture into the center of the room and began covering them and the floor with tape, plastic and paper. They paraded back and forth through the house and out the front door all day. Beaux Bo thought they were there to play with him, so guess who had to hold and/or play with him all day and make sure he didn't run out the front door. The painter shut down about dark and said he would be back the next morning and finish up in a few hours. Ah, things would be back to normal for a while and I could relax.

Well, I needed to take a shower. Guess who never thought about getting all the essentials out of our bedroom and bathroom before it was all hidden under a mountain of plastic, paper and tape. Therefore, I was given a mission. Go into the battleground, locate and secure the necessary supplies to get us through the night: underwear, toothbrushes, clothes for the next day, etc. I kissed Amber and went in. I crawled, I was on my back, stomach, side, knees doing all I could to maneuver through the maze of crap. I mean, "our lovely furnishings". Everything looked different. When I did reach the drawer I needed, I couldn't get it open, so in a twisted position on the floor I had to push, pull and strain just to move things enough to get my hand in enough to pull out a pair of underwear. (If I wasn't already pretty sure I could never father another child, I am certain now). After what seemed like an eternity, I emerged from what used to be our bedroom, battered, bruised and certainly sterile. I proudly held up all that I had gathered in celebration of my return. Amber's smile turned to a smirk and she said, "I don't wear those anymore!"

I've Been Thinkin'

It was as if we were staying in a hotel room. Different room, different bed (And different side of the bed for some reason), different bathroom, different everything! First, the shower in the guest bath was too small. I kept hitting my elbows on the walls, and the acoustics for singing were dreadful. Plus, I had left all the good reading material in the other bathroom. Finally we went to bed. Beaux Bo was totally confused and a nervous wreck. He ran from one side of the bed to the other all night long because Amber and I were sleeping on the wrong side of the bed and it just blew his routine all to heck.

The bed made strange noises every time we (or Beaux Bo) moved. The ceiling fan didn't have the familiar hum as the one in our room but instead had an obnoxious rhythmic click. There was a single beam of light finding its way through the shades and hitting me in my left eye. But, despite all obstacles, I apparently fell asleep for a minute, and when the call of nature came, I jumped from the bed and walked right square into the wall. I couldn't find the light switch and was able to avoid embarrassment by mere seconds as I skidded into the bathroom. Other than that, it wasn't a bad night.

The next day was pretty much the same as the day before – tarps, plastic, paper and tape everywhere, painter and wife marching in and out of the house, etc. On this day, however, there was the strong smell of paint which gave me a headache and apparently caused Beaux Bo to begin a vomiting binge that involved several rooms. A much deserved "thank you" goes out to Amber for cleaning up the mess due to the fact I was outside with Beaux Bo getting some fresh air at the time.

Dennis, the painter, finally finished, gathered up all their tarps and stuff, collected his check and prepared to leave. I guess he saw me standing with my mouth open looking around at the thousands of white specks left over from the old popcorn finish in our bedroom ceiling, the dust and various other debris scattered all over the house. He paused and asked if we wanted him and his wife to clean up a little around the house. Just as I was about to yell, "Hell yes!", Amber softly says she appreciates the offer, but that we would do it ourselves. Oh well, the football games weren't that good anyway.

We began. We worked. We worked and worked and worked. We dusted, vacuumed, swept and mopped on and under everything in the house.

I saw parts of this house I had never seen before in the twenty-five years we had lived there. We stopped to eat, but everything tasted like paint. I just couldn't get that smell out of my head. Finally, around midnight, Amber said that's good enough and we headed for bed. We would again have to sleep in the guest bedroom, but I was so tired I figured I would have no problem sleeping that night. Wrong!! (See the previous paragraph starting with, "The bed made strange noises...".)

We rolled out of bed early the next morning (I wasn't asleep anyway), eager to get our bedroom back in order now that the paint was dry. We walked into the room and as I prepared to attack and move the pile of furniture back to their original locations, Amber said, "Wait a minute, I'm thinking..."

My thoughts at that moment: "CRAP!! Here we go!"

She decided this would be a good chance to change and rearrange the room. I moved the king-size bed from one wall to another before she decided its new location. I'm just glad there are only four walls in that room or I might still be moving the bed. We then moved the thousand pound (seemed like) dressers like we were playing a chess match. We again dusted, vacuumed and cleaned everything in the bedroom. Amber said we could quit sometime after dark, saying we would hang all her pictures and knickknacks later. We were able to shower and sing in our own bathroom and sleep in our bedroom that night.

It has now been four days, or has it been a month, since this all began, and we are back to normal. Sure, I still have to hang all the stuff on the walls, food still tastes like paint, I'm still getting up at night and walking into walls because the bed isn't where it is supposed to be, and it takes me forever to get dressed because I can't remember where my underwear, socks and t-shirts are now located.

Yep, nothing's where it's s'posed to be, and maybe it wasn't all that quick and easy, but when I see the smile on my sweet Amber's face, I know it was good.

I've Been Thinkin'

I BLAME THE ROAD

Ya' know, there are certain roads that seem to draw more idiots than others. In my area, there are two highways in particular that make me cringe every time I must navigate them: 1187 and 174. I'm talking roads that have 55 and 60 MPH speed limits but attract folks (I'm trying not to use the word "idiots") that drive 35 and 40 in both lanes, most times side by side. It's like they have this instinct, knowing when I'm on these roads and then as if driven by one common brain (I use that term figuratively) they form impenetrable moving roadblocks.

I saw a program the other night that was discussing a smog-absorbing cement that was being used on some roads in large traffic areas. I'm thinking there is some kind of chemical make-up within these two roads that attracts idiots - I'm sorry, "morons" - I'm sorry again! It's probably something like the smell of flowers attracting bees. If we must use these chemicals in roads, then I feel part of the driving test should be to test every potential driver with these chemicals and if these nuts (sorry) fail by reacting, well, like idiots, they will not be allowed to drive.

To be fair, each idiot (I know) should be sent to rehab to teach them to cope with these idiotic urges. If, after an appropriate amount of time they are still an idiot when exposed to these chemicals, then they will be sent to live in Cut and Shoot, Texas for as long as they might live.

Do more than listen to the words, hear their meaning. Do more than offer your hand, share your heart. Do more than see their pain, embrace their cause. Do more than simply live your life; dream for a better life for all. Unselfish existence...it matters.

I've Been Thinkin'

THE STRENGTH OF SILENCE

―――◆―――

We took a deep breath, gritted our teeth, ducked our heads and said goodbye to the safety and comfort of home, and set out for our first attempt living life away from the security of family, friends and familiarity. The grand old Santa Fe Railroad had seen fit to promote me to my first management job to be headquartered in Temple, Texas, so this old home boy who had always figured he'd spend the rest of his life in his hometown of Brownwood, Texas, or possibly Cleburne, Texas, his wife's home town, was off to a place where they would have no family or friends. I always felt confident of every job or position that I had worked and this was no different. However, this time my family would be involved in the adjustments, and that made me nervous. It was scary.

To add to the uneasiness of uprooting the family and settling in an area unfamiliar to us, both socially and physically, there was also this thing about buying our first house. New job, new people, new area, new house... this was going to be interesting. In our favor were the kids, Shanon and Shaye, who were young enough to uproot and resettle with minimum adjustment, I was also confident in my abilities on the new job and in the Santa Fe Railway Company. Probably the most important advantage was the strength and never yielding support of my sweet wife, Amber. The commitment was made and in August, 1978, in the middle of a black land corn field in Academy, Texas, ten miles south of Temple, concrete was poured and the first nails driven at the site that would be our home for the next ten years.

Our new neighborhood was part of a new development comprised of families with a lot in common with us. They were young, living in their first home and new to the area. We quickly met most all the neighbors with the exception of the family that lived right next door to us. They seemed friendly; they always smiled and waved, but they never spoke. After a week or so some of the other neighbors informed us that our next door neighbors were hearing impaired. I had never been around anyone without hearing, other than I could recall as a child people stopping by the house as they went door to door. They would give Mom a card saying they were deaf and asking her to buy pencils for whatever she wanted to pay for them. I was at a loss as to what to do, but several more weeks passed with friendly waves and a smile as we would see each other coming and going from our respective homes.

Finally, I decided enough was enough. I wasn't going to live next door to someone and not communicate. I saw him open his garage and walk inside, so I headed that way. I approached the open garage, I became uneasy because I had no idea how I was going to communicate with my neighbor. As I entered the garage doorway, he stood with his back to me working on his boat. I stopped in my steps. I certainly didn't want to frighten him. Even more uneasy, I decided to just stand there until he turned around. It seemed like an eternity. My mind was racing, was I standing too close, was I going to startle him, should I move farther out in the driveway? Then he finally turned my way. Not startled at all, his face lit up into a huge smile and he walked toward me with his hand extended.

His handshake was firm and deliberate. He was a big man with medium length blond hair, weathered tan skin, and a confident smile that made me feel at ease. I smiled and said, "Hello!" He raised his hand to me and waved. He then pointed to his ears and shook his head in a negative gesture. I nodded in the affirmative and said slowly, "My name is Terry, I live next door," and pointed to my house. He then nodded and pointed to me, then my house. He then placed his hand on my shoulder and gestured for me to wait where I was, and he walked into his house.

He quickly returned with a pencil and a pad, and handed them to me. He had written, "Hi! My name is Wayne. What did you say your name was?"

That's the way our first conversation and friendship began. We communicated in the beginning, writing notes and using a modified form of Charades, something I never really liked, mostly because I wasn't very good at it. We laughed and joked, and before much time passed I felt comfortable around Wayne. He had a way of making you feel comfortable. He was very confident and if anything, I was the one who felt challenged because of my inept ability to communicate well with him. At one point he reached over and grabbed my full mustache and pulled it upward. He then wrote a note saying he could read lips fairly well unless your lips are hidden behind a huge mustache, laughing as he handed me the note.

He asked if I had ever been around the deaf before and I indicated that I hadn't except those that would come by my house when I was a child selling pencils. He shook his head and quickly wrote that there was nothing wrong with his hands, arms, legs or his brain. He said that he could work as hard as anyone and did not need sympathy. He concluded the subject by telling me that if anyone ever came by my house claiming to be deaf, asking for a hand out, send them to his house. First he would find out real quick if they were indeed deaf, and if they were, he would tell them where to get a job.

Later, I met his lovely wife Barbara. She too was an intelligent, beautiful, energetic lady with a tremendous sense of humor. I loved watching them communicate. Their signing was so rhythmic and beautiful to watch. You could see and feel the emotion in their conversations. You could see the love they had for one another. They took the time to explain to Amber and me that they had both been born without the ability to hear. They explained that they had the ability to speak, but never received the proper education as to how to talk verbally. Their three year old daughter could hear and speak and it was amazing to watch her sign at such a young age. It was funny watching Wayne scolding his young daughter using sign language and seeing her cross her little arms and turn her back to ignore his angry signing and then see him smile, walk closer to her and thump the back of her ear, and tell her to pay attention to what he was saying, much the same as the conversations between me and my two young daughters.

It didn't take long for our two families to become close. We spent more and more time together. Wayne was a heck of a bass fisherman and began teaching me his fishing secrets. Our communication was getting better (My Charades skills were improving), but it still took too long on my part. One evening there was a knock on my door and when I opened it, there stood Wayne. He handed me a book titled "Sign Language Made Simple", along with a note saying, "Terry, I am giving you this book as a friend. I think you have a lot to say, as I do. After doing some thinking, I figured it would be easier for you to learn how to sign than for me to learn how to hear."

Amber and I worked hard learning to sign, even practicing signing to each other. We became fairly proficient even to the point where we would sign to each other at night when the kids were in bed to keep them from hearing us. We never gained the poetic like gestures that Wayne and Barbara possessed, but we were mechanically sound. It was nice to be able to say something meaningful and lengthy to Wayne without having to run down a pen and paper. For the most part, our friendship was as natural as it would have been with anyone.

There were still adjustments made as our friendship grew, and Amber and I were made to appreciate a lot of things we had always taken for granted. Wayne and I became fishing partners. Most times we would get an early start, around five o'clock in the morning. There were several mornings I would wake up, get dressed and sit outside waiting for Wayne for long periods of time. I knew that their doorbell was hooked up to the lights in certain rooms of their house but not the bedrooms, so, after trying the doorbell a couple of times, I would just lean against the car and wait. Wayne would eventually stagger out the door, tell me he was sorry and we would be off on our fishing trip. He explained that his wakeup alarm was a small strobe light, but if he was facing the wrong way and the light was not flashing directly into his face, it would not wake him up and certainly not wake up his wife.

One day after one of these late wakeup incidents, Wayne gave me a key to his house. He explained that in the future when he was late rising, he wanted me to use the key and come in and wake him up. I told him that I appreciated his trust, but that I would feel uncomfortable having a key and entering his house with them asleep inside. He smiled and explained that it wasn't just for waking him for fishing trips. He continued by saying that he trusted me as a friend and that he would sleep better knowing that a hearing person had the ability to wake and/or notify him and his family if there was a reason to evacuate the house.

I agreed, and showing his amazing sense of humor, he said it would probably be best not to give him a key to our house because at night and in the dark, if he had reason to enter our house, he would not be able to hear me say, "Stop, or I will shoot!"

A few days later we had another planned early morning fishing trip. As I had feared, he was late. I walked to his front door, pushed the doorbell button a couple of times with no response, and finally used the key. I turned on the living room light and there was nothing. I called out thinking maybe Addie, their little girl, would hear me and there was nothing. I slowly walked to the hall, turning on the light, then to their bedroom door and, before looking inside the bedroom, reached inside the door and turned the light switch off and on a few times. Then I slowly peeked inside. Barbara, who was facing me, raised up, smiled, waved and sent an elbow into Wayne's side. With a groan, he raised to one elbow, waved and started his bed dismount. With that, I was out of there.

There are so many things I would like to share about Wayne and Barbara: their unbelievable lives, sense of humor, silent strengths and the growth Amber and I were fortunate enough to go through in the years we shared with them. I still smile when I think of Wayne and his beautiful wife coming over and spending the evening cooking out, laughing and visiting. Wayne would walk in, sit on the couch, and if I had the stereo on, would begin to tap his foot and nod his head to the beat of the music. He would turn to me and see the surprised look on my face, smile and sign, "I can hear now!", then laugh, reach over and slap me on the knee and explain that he could feel the vibrating beat from the speakers. There were times when he and Barbara would embrace and dance to the beat of the music.

After hours of fun and laughter they would go home and in conversation with Amber, I would relate that Wayne had said they were going to Houston the next weekend to visit some of his family. Amber would pause and say Barbara had indicated they were going to Austin the next weekend to visit with her folks. In situations like this we were never sure if Wayne and Barbara just hadn't communicated to each other yet, or if one or both of us had misunderstood their signing to us.

For most of our married life, Amber and I have enjoyed some of our best and most informative conversations after we have turned off the lights and have gone to bed. We sum up the day's activities, discuss future plans, bills and make sure we are on the same page prior to going into the next day. With Wayne and Barbara, once the lights went off, there wasn't but a few things they could do, and talking was not one of them.

For someone who had a disability (Don't ever let Wayne know I said that.) Wayne was amazing. I would hear a squadron of helicopters from Ft. Hood fly overhead and walk outside to see them and Wayne would walk outside and look to the sky, then wave to me, smile and sign, "Boy, that was loud!". Then there was the day I had bought a new metal detector and was out in the yard trying it out. Wayne came home from work and walked over to see what I was up to. After explaining to him how the detector would buzz when I passed over something metal, he insisted on trying it. He closed his eyes and I pitched a quarter out into the yard and told Wayne it was somewhere in the front yard. Within minutes he passed over the quarter, the detector buzzed, he stopped, reached down and picked up the quarter, turned, held up the quarter and with a big smile signed, "That's easy!" I asked how he did it, and with a sly smile on his face he said he could hear now, then admitted he could feel the vibration in his hand.

Fishing with Wayne was amazing. It was astonishing how he could always find the fish. Driving to the lake, Wayne would always observe the cattle in pastures along the way. He claimed if the cattle are eating, then the fish were biting. He also claimed he could smell the fish when asked how he always caught his limit. We would be out on the lake when all of a sudden his nose would raise toward the sky and he would turn to me and ask if I could smell it. Of course, to me, the lake always smelled like a lake, but sure enough, he would crank up the boat motor and within a few minutes we would be hauling in the fish. He claimed that baitfish gave off a smell when larger fish chased them toward the surface, but like I said, it always just smelled like lake water to me.

If I needed to get Wayne's attention while fishing, I would just tap the bottom of the boat with my foot. He would immediately turn to me and ask what I wanted, then remind me that I was scaring the fish.

If we were in Wayne's boat and he was operating the trolling motor, (When bass fishing, the person in the front of the boat usually has the first and best shot at catching fish.) every once in a while he would turn to me and ask, "What did you just call me?" Of course I would deny I had said anything, even though I may have, and Wayne would claim that he heard me, then smile, knowing he made me feel uneasy.

I was a member of a bowling team that Santa Fe sponsored and we bowled every Thursday night. We weren't very good, but we sure had a good time. One day I was getting ready to leave to bowl, and one of my teammates called to say he wasn't going to make it. As I walked out to the car, Wayne drove up and walked over to visit. I told him I was going to bowl but we were going to be short a bowler so we were going to forfeit the match. Wayne said he would be happy to go if they would let him bowl. I asked if he had ever bowled in a league and he said he had, but it had been a while. I told him not to worry about it because we just bowled for the fun of it, that we seldom ever won a game. We arrived, I introduced Wayne to my teammates, Wayne found a ball, rented some shoes and we were on our way.

It was unbelievable. We, or I guess I should say Wayne, won every game. Wayne bowled 220, 248 and 265, then apologized for not bowling as well as he should, saying he probably would have done better if he had brought his own ball and shoes. Everyone liked him and it was amazing how fast Wayne could win people over. The guys invited him to stay, shoot some pool and drink a few beers. He thanked them and said he didn't drink, but would stay and shoot pool. I don't think he lost a game. We had a good time and when we were through, Wayne asked for my keys and drove us home.

There are so many amazing stories about Wayne and his family, but this is a short story, not a book. I tell this story to share our amazing friendship, and the valuable lessons we learned along the way. Yes, I walked up behind him that first day feeling uneasy, and feeling some amount of pity for this man of silence. Little did I know it was me that would benefit most from our friendship. Wayne and Barbara never hesitated but always dove head on into life and every obstacle it had to offer. I am a better man because of Wayne.

It's been twenty-five years since I last saw Wayne, but his strength still plays a part in a lot of decisions I make and how I look at life. If anything, those ten years we spent with Wayne and Barbara are more valuable now than then. You see, Amber is losing her hearing. She has completely lost her hearing in her left ear and has less than fifty percent hearing in her right ear and there is nothing that can be done about it at this point. But we have seen the strength of silence. We have seen the happiness that strength can bring. Love, and the silent strength of that love, trumps all.

THE ROCK

Beginning back in the early to mid 1960's, one of the favorite pastimes of the Beck clan was going out in the country to an old farm about eight miles south of Brownwood going toward Indian Creek. It was a beautiful place with a little of everything to offer. There were rocky hills, several stock ponds, a creek and a good mixture of trees. There were also signs that there had once been a small settlement on the property, although all that remained were small sections and pieces of a rock fence.

We would hunt, fish, explore, do a little frog gigging and sometime spend all day there and not do anything but maybe eat. Even as I grew older and started figuring out that there were other things in life other than fishing and hunting (namely girls and making the drag with my running buddies) I still enjoyed my times with the family out in the country.

My dad really enjoyed strolling around on the old farm. While we were fishing, horsing around or fighting, Pop would find himself a walking stick and off he would go. As he walked, he would poke and prod at rocks and pieces of flint looking for Indian arrowheads. He found hundreds of them over the years. Another thing that he found was a huge flat rock with a perfectly round hole through the middle of it. Pop would get excited every time he found even a partial arrowhead, so you can imagine how excited he was about this huge rock of several hundred pounds that obviously had some history behind it.

Every trip out to the old farm Pop would walk out and check his rock. Then one day somebody (I don't remember which of us) suggested that we load the rock up and bring it home. I can remember Pop saying that he didn't really think we would be able to accomplish such a task, although you could tell by the smile on his face that we were going to try. My dad, my four brothers and I headed to the farm in Pop's 1949 Chevy pickup. We could only get to within seventy-five yards or so of the rock because of the rough terrain. Without going into the tiring details, we eventually carried the rock to the pickup and loaded it into the bed. For good measure, we also loaded a couple more big rocks, although there wasn't anything special about them other than they were terribly heavy.

It seems like it took forever to get the rocks home. There was so much weight in the bed of the old '49 pickup that every time Pop would hit a bump, the front end of the truck would come off the ground and he would lose the ability to steer. The terrain was so rough on the farm, a couple of us had to ride on the front fenders of the truck to keep the tires on the ground as Pop eased along the old farm trail. Although we were being extremely careful, I suspect that if we were to have done this with today's way of seeing things, Pop would have ended up in jail for child endangerment.

Although it was a long slow trip, we made it home with the rock. We dug a hole and stood the rock up on its edge along with the other rocks we had brought along for company. Over the years we had several really smart people tell us that the rock was a variation of an Indian grind stone. Just to make sure, we also asked a couple of people who weren't quite as smart, and they agreed that the rock was indeed some type of an Indian grind stone.

The rock stood at that location for about fifteen years until Mom and Pop decided to remodel the old house and add on a couple of rooms. It was moved around to the front of the house and there it stood until April 3, 2010. I just could not bear the thought of leaving The Rock behind to live with strangers. My brother Pat met me there and we loaded it in my pickup and transported it to my home in Burleson.

After my Mom passed away, I began to go through hundreds of family photographs. I was amazed how many of the photos had The Rock in them. Sometime it would just be quietly in the background and other times it would be the main backdrop for a photo. The Rock was there for about forty-five years and had a way of letting its presence be known. On August 19, 2002 I took several photographs of Mom, Pop and the brothers. On August 27, 2002, Pop died. The last photo taken of Pop, he was sitting in front of The Rock - his rock. On August 27, 2009 Mom died and some of the last photos of her were taken as she sat in the same chair that Pop had sat in, and yes, she was sitting in front of The Rock - Pop's rock.

After spending four years abiding in our Burleson yard, The Rock made its way with me and Amber to Mills County in 2014, and is now on display for all to see at our Lake Merritt home, where it still serves as a focal point for photos of friends and family.

Someone (Me) once said, "Anyone with half a brain could put that together." Then someone else (Amber) said, "Well, fortunately for us, that plays right into one of your strong points."

I've Been Thinkin'

AMBER GOES FISHING

I have always loved to fish. I was raised in a family of fishermen. My dad, four brothers and yes, even my Mother, spent a lot of time baiting a hook. Back in the "Home" days we did a lot of river and lake fishing, mostly on Lake Brownwood and on the Colorado River, down close to Indian Creek. We ran trot lines in the Pecan Bayou. We also spent a lot of time fishing stock ponds, one of my Dad's favorite locations. At stock ponds, Pop would start out fishing with us, but would almost always end up walking the fields and pastures looking for and finding Indian arrowheads.

Even in my runnin' and gunnin' days after leaving home, I always found time to fish. After getting married and moving to Little River/Academy, just south of Temple, Texas, we were fortunate to have wonderful country neighbors. The couple that lived next door to us were both deaf and even though they had the ability, wouldn't speak. They taught us sign language and we became close friends. Turns out that he was an avid bass fisherman, and it didn't take long for him to convince me to tag along with him and begin to learn about bass fishing on Lake Belton.

It wasn't long before I bought a bass boat and bass fishing became my second love, my wife and kids being my first love. I was in fishing heaven; my boss loved to fish and we did, a lot. I had several close friends that had boats and loved to fish, and I could hook up to my boat at the house and be fishing in Lake Belton in twenty-five minutes when work would allow. The only thing missing was my wife, Amber. I could not convince her that fishing was something she needed to be doing.

Lake Belton was a beautiful lake that wound its way through colorful high rock cliffs and the absence of docks and houses built right down by the shore made the lake more peaceful and natural. I loved the way I felt when on the lake and if I caught a few fish along the way it was just that much better. While I didn't mind, on occasion, fishing by myself I really enjoyed the comradeship of a fishing buddy that had the same respect and admiration of the lake as me.

It became my goal to get Amber out on the lake and eventually become my fishing buddy. I began to tell her all the great things about fishing. She sank that idea quickly when she said that she just didn't have the urge to go out and catch them poor fish out of the lake. I responded by explaining that there was a lot more to fishing than just catching fish. I told her that there was nothing more peaceful and beautiful than slipping the boat into the calm lake waters before the sun came up and slowly gliding through the cool fresh air. I went on by saying there was nothing more enjoyable than being on the lake and watching the world wake up as the sun began to rise above the scenic bluffs. I spoke of getting to see the deer coming down to the water's edge and watching the water birds as they began to stir and look for breakfast. I went on to say that she wouldn't have to fish; she could sit on the back fishing deck, read a favorite book and catch some sun.

I finally convinced her to give it a try. On the morning of our fishing trip, Amber got up at 4:00am so that she could fix her hair and put on her makeup. (I know you are expecting me to make a remark about this, but I'm not.) We arrived at the lake about thirty minutes before sunrise and slipped the boat into the water. We eased across the water toward one of my favorite and most scenic fishing holes. The water was like glass, the air was cool and vibrant. I looked over at Amber and could see a slight smile in the dim dawn light. We arrived at our destination and all we had to do was wait for enough light to begin the day. It was going to be perfect.

About that time there was a clap of thunder and a fierce rain downpour. I had moved to the front fishing platform and Amber had moved to the rear platform. I jumped down and began trying to dig out the rain gear. I retrieved the gear and handed it to Amber. As I turned toward her

I could see her wet hair hanging on her shoulders. There were large black streaks of mascara running down her cheeks, She looked up at me and in a pitiful voice said, "What good is that going to do me now?"

The sun never did come out. We were both a little cool because of the wet clothes, but somehow I did convince Amber that we should at least fish a little while since we were there. She told me that she didn't know how to cast the lure. I told her not to worry, that I had the boat far enough from the bank that she could try to cast as hard as she wanted and wouldn't have to worry about getting hung up in the brush along the bank. After having to pull the boat to the shore and climb a couple of trees to retrieve Amber's lure, we decided it was time to go home.

When we arrived back at the boat ramp there were several other groups of people either putting in or loading up to leave. Amber made me keep my distance until the people cleared out because she didn't want anyone to see her looking like that. Just between you and me, I think she looked cute. Anyway, after staying in a holding pattern for another thirty minutes we finally loaded the boat on the trailer and went home.

There were several lessons learned that day, one of which was not to trust the local TV weatherman. Amber also made something else clear. She didn't mind my fishing as much as I wanted to, as long as I was careful and having a good time... and there was a shopping mall or craft shop available for her and the girls.

It would seem to me that if your feelings toward someone falter when their feelings toward you falter, the feelings you had for each other weren't worth that much to begin with.

SIMPLY FRIENDS

———◆———

While "friend" is singular in its form, it takes at least two to make it so.

And what, pray tell, is a good friend? Is there such a thing as a bad friend?

Why do we belittle some friends by introducing another to them as my best friend?

Old friend: Is that someone who has been your friend for a long time, or is that person just old?

Girlfriend or Boyfriend: Does friend have to be gender specific or will "This is my friend Linda." or "This is my friend Bob." work just fine?

To me there is no greater honor than to be considered someone's friend.

My wife and I were friends long before we were lovers and even more importantly, we are still friends after thirty-seven years of being lovers.

Let "friend" stand as is; a position of honor, trust and loyalty.

There is no need to dilute the term with classifications, degrees or clarifications.

Simple is good----This is my friend.

A friendly look,
a kindly smile,
one good act,
and life's worthwhile.

I've Been Thinkin'

PART OF ME IS YOU

As we make life's journey from beginning to end, the people and places that we visit along the way become a part of us. The miracle of birth gave us our beginning with a microscopic map of how we would develop physically. This map was provided by our mother and our father, and their parents, and their parents' parents. This physical part of our development follows a prearranged path influenced from time to time by outside forces and fads.

It is my belief that the growth and development of our inner self is a little more complicated, and less predestined. As we move down life's rambling road, we incur relationships with a multitude of other individuals who are themselves traveling along their path to their final destination.

Love of a simple life with respect for others came to me from my grandparents. A respect for nature and its animal inhabitants, and the joy brought by country living came from my cousins. A love of my God and the strength He provides was given to me by my pastors and other faithful followers. I carry with me the healthy competitiveness that drives me to be the best, while honoring my teammates as well as my competitors, as taught by my coaches and teachers.

I have known love from the beginning of my journey: love of my Mother and Father and my brothers four. I learned of a different love as I entered my teenage years. A part of how I feel about and respect romantic love was implanted by the girls who won my heart and shared a newfound form of this emotion. Now I have learned the greatest lesson in love, and to Amber, my sweet wife, I will always be thankful.

I carry within me bits and pieces of everyone I have known; the friends, the bosses, co-workers, teammates, coaches and loving family members. My inner development will continue as I meet new souls or become reacquainted with old friends. Within this worn and graying shell, there live the memories of many, guiding the acts of one simple man. My hope is that I will represent them well, or that they will forgive me if I don't.

I've Been Thinkin'

THE NIGHT EVERYTHING CHANGED

The moon rested atop the trees as its reflection streaked across the lake.

They sat in the car with windows down. The cool night air brought with it the freshness of the late night.

She moved across the seat, raised his arm and cuddled next to him as she lowered his arm across her shoulders.

He looked down at her soft face and he could see the purple light of the stereo player reflecting in her eyes as she looked up at him with a tender, sweet smile.

He turns his head and again looks across the water as he feels a tightening in his throat and a terrible lump begins to form.

He takes a deep breath and again looks down at her sweet face, taking his finger and brushing her hair from her forehead and says, "We need to talk".

He felt her squeeze his arm and say, as she buried her face in his chest, "No we don't, please, no!"

He knew he had to say what he needed to say now. It wasn't going to get any easier. He had been consumed for days, battling with himself over the right thing to do.

They had been together longer than he had been with anyone for awhile. She was a wonderful person; quiet, witty, very patient and beautiful.

But in years past he had given his heart to others that he thought he would spend the rest of his life with, only to be left broken hearted.

Although some of his concern may have been selfish, he cared for her deeply and he knew that she would do anything for him.

He didn't know if he would ever be ready to settle down, and she had already been hurt badly, much more so than he could have imagined going through himself. He didn't want to be the cause of more pain.

Had he waited too long? Had he been so selfish and involved in his own feelings and history that things had already developed well past his intended state of emotion?

He could still feel her tight grip on his arm and feel the dampness of her tears on his chest. It seemed as if they had been sitting there for hours as he cleared his throat and placed his hand on the side of her face.

Although he still felt the tightness in his throat and was fighting back tears of his own, he gathered his thoughts and summoned the strength to speak.

Before he could get the first word out of his mouth, she reached up, placed her hands on either side of his face, wiped a tear from his cheek with her thumb, smiled and said, "I love you."

His mind cleared, his past was gone, and everything seemed so simple as he smiled back and said, "I love you, too."

I'M NOT THAT KIND OF GUY

I love music. I don't need a crowd to enjoy music. As matter of a fact, it's most enjoyable when I am by myself or with a few close friends or family members, as long as they share my attachment for good music. I often dream of having the ability to sing or play a musical instrument, to be able to pick up a guitar or sit at a piano and play or sing whatever my heart feels. I have owned a guitar since I was twelve years old and my only accomplishment was to prove I'm not the musical kind.

I love art. I envy those who can transcribe what their heart and eyes see into a beautiful display of art. To possess the natural ability to take nothing but a thought and talent and turn it into something beautiful and loved by many is a wondrous thing. I've made many attempts in artistic ventures only to confirm that it is also not one of my natural abilities. I'm afraid I'm not the artsy kind.

I love sports. I have participated in some form of sporting competition since I was six years old. I have played baseball, football, basketball, golf, tennis, volleyball, racquetball and participated in dozens of other athletic ventures, always working hard and long hours. Although I dreamed of college scholarships and even becoming a professional of some kind, the best I could muster was average, and most times maybe a little below. I guess I just never was the naturally athletic kind.

I loved my job. Although I would have preferred having a business of my own, and to have reaped the benefits brought in by my unique business abilities, I soon found that my destiny would be to always work for the other man. I was ambitious and worked my way up the corporate ladder only to spend the last few years working my way back down that same ladder. It seems that my goals, not necessarily my ambitions, had changed. I was not the hardcore business-minded kind.

I have always loved literature, although I would never have admitted it in my younger days. I have always been amazed at those who could take the words that we use every day and transform them into a beautiful and memorable piece of literature, whether it be poetry or any of the many forms of literary expression. I spend a lot of time reading pieces and then thinking, "Man, I wish I'd said that!" The hard fact is that I am just a guy who loves to BS and will occasionally put it in writing. I'm the first to admit that I'm not really the literary kind.

I love my family and friends. When I was young I dreamed of finding the people with whom I would share my life. I was raised with love and had a deep need for sharing that love. I am proud of my family. I am proud of my friends. There have been many dreams and hopefully there will be many more. However, the things that mean the most to me are my family and friends, and they are part of my proudest moments. I am comfortable with my abilities and accomplishments. I have learned that you don't have to be a musician to enjoy music, be an artist to enjoy art, be an accomplished athlete to enjoy sports, or be a published writer or poet to enjoy literature. You do have to be true to those you love and respect if you are going to be a good family man and friend.

And that's the kind of guy I want to be.

I've Been Thinkin'

IT'S A BEAUTIFUL DAY IN THE NEIGHBORHOOD

My purpose for being outside was to start cleaning out the flowerbeds in the front yard. I would like to say I was there to perform a more manly chore; however, my body pretty much dictates the degree of manliness involved in my chores and today it was saying "flowerbeds". It was not really cold outside but not really warm either, and the wind seemed to be kind of irritating. There are some rather large boulders bordering a large Red Oak containing the flowerbed I had chosen to begin working on. I kneeled down near the large rocks and then my knees decided it would be much more comfortable to just sit flat on my butt. As I sat and leaned back against the rocks, I kind of nestled between them and all of a sudden I felt comfortable.

Being close to the ground I could no longer feel the irritating effects of the wind but I could feel the calming heat of the sun. For the moment, cleaning out the flowerbed was on hold. My old body said, "I am comfortable, this is nice". As I sat there, a flurry of leaves blew past me heading south. I thought I recognized several of them from a bunch of northbound leaves the day before. As I sat there protected by my rocky abode, I looked down the street and thought how beautiful our little neighborhood street is, or at least it would be if it weren't for all the garbage bags and boxes sitting out at the curb. It was garbage day.

I could hear the wind blowing through the leafless limbs of the great Red Oak above me as I peered up into the bright blue sky. It was blessedly tranquil until it was interrupted by the scraping noise of a large cardboard box being blown from someone's garbage pile down the street at about 10 to 15 mph. Then it stopped directly in front of my house and just sat there even though the wind had not let up. I sat there thinking "Crap". I was going to have to go out and accept responsibility for someone else's trash. Then, just as I had about given up hope, the box began to move again and I had to resist waving goodbye as the rogue box had just become someone else's problem.

As I sat there drifting closer to an unscheduled nap, I heard such a clatter I had to sit up to see what was the matter. It was an aluminum foil pie pan flipping down the street like a lame Frisbee. Then about fifty feet behind the pie pan was a twelve inch square of Styrofoam coming down the street being chased by the sports section of yesterday's Fort Worth Star Telegram. It was going to be a close race to the corner but the Styrofoam got lodged behind the neighbor's mailbox and the sports page won going away. You know how Styrofoam is. It's just not the smartest or the most athletic when it comes to trash.

I sat there, kind of caught up in the beauty of nature and the sounds of trash blowing by my house, when the neighbor from across the street, a young police officer, came walking out in his yard and gave me a holler. He said he was just checking on me, but probably was making sure I hadn't passed out in the front yard. I assured him I was fine. He put his handcuffs back in his pocket and went back in the house.

I leaned back for one more look into God's beautiful sky. I breathed the cool fresh air that seemed to clear my mind and put me at ease as I looked upward. Then, as though punctuating an end to a perfect morning, I could see the almost effortless flight of a mighty eagle as it rode the wind currents. It came closer and I was awed at its majesty. I felt a sense of pride as he flew overhead and…began to circle…well crap!

It's a dang buzzard, and he thinks he's found lunch!

So much for nature in the neightborhood…

I've Been Thinkin'

STAGE I WATER RESTRICTIONS – BURLESON, TEXAS

Beginning August 29th, Burleson will begin Stage I water restrictions. These restrictions will remain in effect for the rest of your natural life, or until we get about eight and one-half feet of rain.

Addresses ending in an odd number will be able to water their lawn or landscape on Sundays and Thursdays except between the hours of 10 AM and 6 PM and 8:25 AM and 9:10 AM and between 7:32 PM and 8:13 PM.

Addresses ending in an even number will be able to water their lawn or landscape on Tuesdays and Saturdays except between the same times as the odd numbered addresses unless using blue or green water hose, which would allow watering during the 7:32 PM - 8:13 PM time frame.

There will be no lawn or landscape watering at all on Mondays. There also will be no flushing of toilets and the brushing of teeth will only be allowed if you are actually going to be in the presence of people other than family.

Except on Mondays, when there will be no toilet flushing, toilet flushing will alternate between odd and even addresses from day to day beginning with odd on Tuesday. It is suggested, if you are not already, that you become closer friends with the neighbor on one side or the other.

Baths and long showers are limited to three times a week and cannot occur on the same day that the lawn was watered or a toilet was flushed and, as with teeth brushing, should only be performed if you are going to be in the presence of someone other than family. Bathing in lawn sprinklers will not be charged as a formal bath or shower, however, adults over fifty years of age are restricted to backyard sprinklers only unless pre-approved by the City Manager.

Car washing will not be permitted unless incorporated with bathing and would also need City Manager's approval. The washing of clothes will be limited to one time every ten days. This shouldn't present a problem, in that putting on clean underwear when you haven't had a shower or bath wouldn't do a lot of good anyway.

Any violations of the above mentioned regulations will result in the following:

- First offense - a warning and a two thousand dollar fine.
- Second offense - ten thousand dollar fine.
- Third offense - four tickets to a Cowboy Game sitting next to Jerry Jones.

PRAY FOR RAIN!!!

I've Been Thinkin'

ONLY GONNA TELL THIS STORY ONCE

My heart had been broken. Again. I had thrown my hands in the air and said "To hell with it all". Again. I was drenched and slowly drowning in my own unique version of self pity. My dreams and my dreamlike world in the small town of Florence, Texas had been shattered, leaving me in a state of utter dumbness. All my plans, my goals, my heart and apparently even most of my intelligence were wiped out by one heartless phone call from the girl I had planned to marry.

About six months earlier, I had decided to leave the warmth and safety of home, my hometown, and all the security attached to those things. After all, I was twenty-one years old, ready to get married and this would be the smart thing to do if I was going to make enough seed money for the big day. (I'll get back to the "smart" part of this later.) There was also a possibility I was growing tired of, or possibly disillusioned with the education process. After all, I had been getting a formal education for almost sixteen years, and I couldn't tell it was making a difference. The fact that I only needed twelve more hours to earn that degree didn't come into the thinking process. (Like I said, we'll talk about this smart thing later.)

I began a job with a hometown company in Brownwood, Texas, that was opening a warehouse in Killeen, Texas. Not liking the idea of adjusting to a bigger town, I found a room to rent in the small town of Florence, about ten miles southwest of Killeen. My landlord, Mr. Williams, was a well renowned widower in the area who quickly won my respect and became almost grandfather-like to me in the six months we shared his home, his farm, his stories and his quiet wisdom. The small town turned out to be the perfect place for me to adjust, grow, and all the while actually save money. I quickly befriended a handful of quiet souls and they helped make this small town a good home away from home. During the weekdays we would eat together, play, fish and with few exceptions shared a quiet, warm and reassuring friendship; Just what I needed to get me through the week until I could get back home on the weekends and reaffirm that the love of my life was worth it.

Then, when I had convinced myself that things could never be any better, I received the call that broke my heart. I can remember the lump that built in my throat and the knot that seemed to squeeze all that mattered from my heart. All of a sudden, nothing was important anymore. Nothing mattered. All of a sudden, this place that had served as my paradise away from home seemed so far away from anything good. I wanted to pack my bags and leave that very moment, but, as far as work was concerned, my daddy didn't raise a quitter, so I gave my notice, and waited to go home.

My final week in Florence arrived. During my time there, I had also become friends with a feller in Killeen who owned and operated a music shop. Jim and I would usually eat lunch together and then I would hang around his store for a while after work, listening to music and shooting the bull. Jim was a little older than me and divorced, so he tried to console me because, while our situations weren't exactly identical, they were close enough that he thought he could help. Jim talked of keeping my mind and body busy. He said that he and some of his buddies from Waco, were going to a club in Austin Tuesday night and it might be just the thing I needed to get my mind on something else. Although hesitant, I finally gave in and agreed to go with them rather than spend another night looking at the four walls of my room and trying not to think.

Tuesday, after work, Jim followed me to my place where we cleaned up, grabbed a quick bite to eat and headed to Austin to meet up with his buddies. The name of the club slips my mind after all these years, but it seems like it had something to do with the sky...Skyline or Skylight? From this point there are a lot of gaps in the timeline as well as assumptions made. I do remember walking into the Club and meeting Jim's friends. I can remember someone ordering drinks. It seems like these drinks involved a big mug of beer, a small shot glass of some kind of hard liquor, dropping the shot glass into the mug of beer (something about a depth charge) and then drinking the concoction rather rapidly. I was later told I didn't last long. I apparently went (waddled) into the restroom (hopefully the men's) and never came back. Jim, and my new friends finally found me trying to hold the commode still while I threw up.

My newfound comrades apparently brought me back to the table and propped me up in a chair for an undetermined amount of time. Later, my buds decided it was time to get a bite to eat, so they carried me out to the car, again propped me up and we were off to find a restaurant. I was left in the car (I assume they were tired of carrying me) while they went in to eat. I finally woke up (or regained consciousness), or at least sort of, and did have the whereabouts to know I needed to potty. I removed myself from the vehicle. Not having the foggiest notion where I was, I started looking for a restroom. As I walked (waddled) through the parking lot, a car with several gals aboard stopped and asked me where the nearest convenience store was. To the best of my ability, I told them I had no idea, that I was looking for a restroom. They told me to hop in and I could go with them to a store. I said, "All righty!" and the saga began.

It seems we drove for a while, but they did find a store and we were all able to take care of our needs. After getting back to the car I suggested that they might ought to take me back to my friends car before they missed me. They said they would be happy too and then said, "How do we get back to the car?" UH-OH!

We drove around for what seemed like hours, and saw nothing familiar. I finally decided that my clubbing buddies were probably long gone or had the police looking for me. I told the equally confused gals to please just find the freeway and I could find my way out of town and hitchhike back home to Florence. Another eternity seemed to pass, but we finally found the freeway. After thanking them, I bid my fellow masters of confusion farewell and I was off on my first attempt at hitchhiking.

Still wobbly, and feeling like I would have to die just to feel some better, I began my quest spending more time turning and sticking my thumb out to every passing vehicle, than actually walking. I had no idea what time it was, not that it mattered. Every hour seemed like an eternity. I had never felt so lonely in the middle of so many people. After a while I began to take the rejection of the passing vehicles personally and finally thought "To hell with it," ducked my head and started to walk as fast and straight as my inebriated concentration could handle. I would glance back every once in a while to see how far I had traveled, only to be disappointed at the meager mileage I had logged. After several eternities, I quit looking back and just marched on, my sweat soaked shirt and dress slacks sticking to my panting body. My huffing and puffing was more of an effort to keep from crying than from fatigue at this point.

Then, without warning, and from out of nowhere, there was a barrage of flashing lights and a booming voice, "Stop walking and move off the shoulder of the highway!" I turned and it looked like there were ten police vehicles behind me (Turns out there was only one.) I moved off the shoulder of the road and again the voice echoed, "Stand where you are with your hands held out where I can see them!" I wasn't lonely anymore. I was scared spitless.

Time began to move in slow motion. It seemed as though I stood in that spot forever before I was finally told to walk slowly toward the car. With about a half dozen spotlights shining on me, it was difficult to see the car, much less if there was anyone out of the car. As I came closer to the car I finally was able to make out the silhouette of the officer standing in front of the vehicle. He began the conversation with a series of simple questions, which was good in that I don't think I could have answered anything that would have taken any concentrated effort on my part. He then asked for some form of identification. I reached for my billfold and slapped nothing but an empty back pocket. My heart stopped. I knew it was gone, but for some reason I gave myself a pat down, slapping all my pockets, front and back. I think I was trying to buy time, because I sure as heck didn't know what to say. My only thought: "Here come the handcuffs!"

Fortunately for me, the officer was taking this situation a lot more calmly than I was. After watching me nearly slap the pockets off my slacks, he finally asked me my name and my address. I told him my name and my Florence address, and was told to stand in front of the car as he sat back in the car and began talking on his radio. After another eternity, he finally stepped out of the car and asked, "Son, is the Florence address on your driver license?" Stuttering now for the first time in my life, I told him that my hometown address in Brownwood, Texas was on my license. He disappeared into the car again and in just a few minutes, he finally turned off all the spotlights and told me to get inside the car. My thought: "Ok, here we go to jail."

After sitting a few minutes, the officer finally spoke, "We received a call about a possible drunk walking on the side of the highway. Do I need to test you, Mr. Beck?"

Not knowing any better, I answered, "Well, about an hour or so ago that would probably have been me, but I feel like I've walked ten miles, and other than not feeling very good, I don't really believe I am drunk now."

There was another long pause. Then he asked me to tell him how I ended up walking down the highway in Austin, Texas, so I told him. I told him the same story I have been telling you. I'm not sure, but it looked like he wanted to laugh. He then asked, "Well, Mr. Beck, were you going to walk all the way to Florence?"

I told him that I was hopeful I would catch a ride. That's when he asked me if I knew that hitchhiking within the city limits was illegal. My thought: "Ok, here we go to jail!"

After several minutes of tapping on his clipboard with his pen, he said he thought I'd had a tough night that probably wasn't over with yet, but that he didn't have many choices. With that, he told me to sit back and we pulled out on the freeway. Things looked bleak. As we drove, my clearing mind wandered back to how happy, content and free I had been only a week ago. My new main thought: "Why am I so stupid?"

We drove forever, not saying a word. Then we pulled over to the shoulder of the road and the officer cleared his throat and said, "Mr. Beck, this is the end of Austin city limits. This is the Lampasas Highway. The cutoff to Florence is about halfway between here and Lampasas. I hope I'm not making a mistake, but if you think you are all right, I'm going to let you out and let you get home however you can. You just be careful, and... well... here, take this old flashlight so you won't get run over."

With these instructions, I shook his hand and thanked him, probably too many times, and stepped out into the fresh night air. I stood there for a while, glad not to be in jail, but thinking, "Now what? Boy, it is dark out here and not much traffic. I wonder what time it is."

I took a deep breath and started walking, my head feeling like a bass drum every time one of my feet hit the ground. I remember thinking that I wished there was more traffic, more people, more noise, more of something other than this dark silence. I needed something to distract me from thinking. Thinking is what got me into this mess. Then there came a distant rumble that broke my descent into no telling what. Then two headlights and the multiple running lights of an eighteen wheeler came over the hill. The closer it came the more it looked like a carnival ride with thousands of lights...what kind of person would be driving something like that? I turned on my flashlight, still undecided if I should try to catch a ride with this diesel powered light show. As he got close, I just couldn't make myself stick the old thumb out. I would wait for the next vehicle. I turned, ducked my head and started walking as the truck blew by me. Then his brake lights came on and he rapidly slowed and pulled over on the shoulder of the road with his hazard lights flashing. What the heck was I going to do now?

I quickly decided that the last thing I wanted to do was to make some trucker mad, so I took another deep breath and started trotting toward the truck. I didn't realize how far ahead of me the truck had stopped. It felt like I was running a quarter mile run and, considering the shape I was in, my innards felt as though they were coming up into my throat. I finally arrived at my destination and reached up for the grab iron on the side of the truck with my trembling hands (They were trembling more because of my apparent withdrawal from the drunken state I had been in rather than from fear, I think.). I opened the door and pulled myself into the seat. The first thing I heard was, "Damn buddy, I almost didn't see you!" He was a man in his mid fifties or so, clean cut, graying hair, and smelled really good. He appeared to be normal as compared to the personality oddities that my poor mind had conjured on the brief jog to the truck.

As he powered up his truck and we pulled back onto the highway slowly picking up speed, he asked where I was headed. I told him I was trying to get back to Florence. He slapped the steering wheel and said,

"Yep, I know right where the cut off to Florence is. I used to cut across there when Killen was on my run. Too bad I'm not going that way tonight, but I can at least get you to the cutoff."

I didn't have to talk much, since he talked as if he hadn't had anybody to talk to in months. I did ask him where he was heading. He told he was heading to Brownwood to deliver half his load and then on to Abilene to unload the rest. I wanted to tell him Brownwood was my home town, but he didn't pause his conversation long enough for me to get in a word. Anyway, it was nice listening to him talk. He was obviously very happy, and happiness to me seemed like such a long time ago. He finally slowed down to catch a breath, and asked me what the heck I was doing out here in the middle of the night. For the second time that night, I started my short-but-getting-longer tale of woe. I had no more than gotten started when he blurted out, "Oops, sorry buddy, but this is your cut off to Florence."

He brought his rig to a stop, we shook hands and I thanked him, again, too many times. As I opened the door to get out, he said, "Well, good luck son. You'll be awful lucky if you see anybody on that road this time of the night, and make sure you keep an eye out for snakes. You know how they like the warm highway at night."

With that, I slid on out to the ground, waved and said thank you one more time, and shoved the door closed. He gunned the engine a couple of times, blew his horn and pulled back out on the highway. I just stood there as he pulled away, and listened to him run through the gears on his moving light show. I stood there until he disappeared over the next hill and then there was silence and there was darkness. I just thought it was dark back at the city limits of Austin.

I finally turned, looked every direction, then headed toward Florence, one step at a time. I felt horrible. My stomach was growling, my head was throbbing, and my feet were already hurting. After walking about a mile, I started to think (I know, we'll talk about this thinking business after a while), I had driven this fifteen miles or so of road several times and it seemed like there were several long curves and jaunts in the road. If a feller could walk a straight line through the country, he might cut several miles off the trip. I convinced myself that I was never going to see anybody on this little highway anyway so I might as well see if I could cut a few miles off the trip. The first time the highway made a jaunt to the left, I climbed the fence and walked straight, figuring I would run back into the highway after a couple of miles as it meandered back my way. The key was to walk straight and remember the highway would always be on the left.

Have you ever tried to walk straight with no moon, no visible landmarks, just pure darkness? This was my first try. I quickly found out that the loafers I was wearing were not hiking boots. It wasn't long until I had grass burrs, prickly pears, and no telling what else clinging to my socks and up to my knees on my slacks. After about fifteen minutes of wandering in the wilderness, I came to a creek and it just so happened this was one of the few creeks that had running water in it. It must have been spring fed (There you go thinking again, Daniel Boone). I walked back and forth for several hundred yards trying to find a place to cross. The narrowest place I could find appeared to be only five or six feet wide. I finally convinced myself that I could jump over it without a problem. Anyway, I used to broad jump farther than this when I was in elementary school.

I backed up about fifty feet or so and began to run, as fast as you can run in slick bottomed loafers, and when I approached the edge of the creek, jumped with all my might. I soared into the night air stretching out with all my might for the other side. And then came the landing, a little over midway across the creek. As I stood there waist deep in the pure spring water, I looked at one bank and then at the other and it became clear, I had misjudged the distance across the creek. I completed my trek across the creek and pulled my tired, wet and now muddy body up on the bank.

I really didn't want to get up. I wanted to just lie there for awhile. Then something crossed my mind...Water Moccasins! The last thing I needed right then was for a Cottonmouth to crawl up my pant leg. I was on my feet and sloshing my way clear of the creek in seconds. There is probably only one thing worse than having grass burrs, prickly pears and all kinds of sticky stuff sticking to your socks and slacks, and that is having all that stuff sticking to your wet socks and wet slacks. Also, It didn't take long for we to figure out that wet loafers are much less comfortable to hike in than dry loafers. I was miserable. However, I wasn't hot any more.

I've Been Thinkin'

I trudged on to the irritating rhythm of my wet loafers squeaking with every step. I was no longer thinking to myself, I was now talking out loud to myself. I would have definitely been offended had anyone else called me the names I was calling myself. Then, in the middle of nowhere, there stood a house. My first thought was to just knock on the door and throw myself at their mercy. Let the chips fall where they may. It would probably have been the smart thing to do if I had found the house before the creek, but now I looked like an escaped convict. I myself probably wouldn't even help someone that looked like me. I decided to quietly bypass the house. As I started around the house, trying to be as quiet and keeping as much distance as possible, I heard this low, gravelly growl. My heart actually stopped as I froze in my steps and slowly turned toward the haunting growl. There in the partial shadows of the security light stood one of the biggest dogs I had ever seen.

I could see that it had a chain hanging down from his collar. Without delay, I began running. My only thought: "how long is that chain?" About the time that I figured he surely was running out of chain, I began hearing a strange hissing noise to go along with the dog's violent barking. I glanced over my shoulder and I could see the other end of the chain was hooked on a clothesline. The hissing sound was the hook sliding down the line as the killer dog closed the distance between us. I felt the dog clip my foot with his paw and I knew the end was near. Just as I had spent the last of my strength and energy, I heard a loud pop and a terrible yelp from the dog as he ran out of clothes line and was jerked backward to the ground. I began to slow down and just as I turned to see the dog, I heard a door slam closed and a man's voice yelling, "What ya got out there, Rocky?"

I didn't look back again. I ran into the thick undergrowth of briars and brush. As I ran, the briars seemed to be grabbing my arms and spinning me around, ripping at my clothes and slapping across my face, but my feet and legs never stopped. I was still running as fast as my sick, worn body would move when I hit a barbed wire fence, partially hidden in the dark by brush and briars. I bounded backward hitting flat on my back, knocking the breath from my lungs. For a moment I thought it was all over. I didn't know if I had been shot, clubbed or electrocuted. Finally, I found the flashlight lying next to me. As I shined it on my chest, I could see the telltale scratches of barbed wire through my torn shirt. I turned off the flashlight, slowly got to my feet, climbed over the fence and slowly walked into the darkness. I didn't care anymore. I was so tired, so sick that, even though I knew I was hurt, I just couldn't feel it anymore...I was numb.

I started walking with nothing on my mind except, "The road is on my left." I didn't care about distances anymore, I didn't care about my appearance...I wanted to go home. Just as the eastern sky began to take on a slight glow, I finally came to another fence and on the other side of that fence was the road and I was still alive. I crawled over the fence and stumbled over to the road's shoulder, ducked my head and started walking toward Florence. I could now feel every bloody blister on my feet, but I didn't stop. I didn't even slow down.

The glow in the eastern sky grew brighter and a cool morning breeze soothed my tattered body and throbbing head. Then the silence was broken, I turned to see an old pickup coming up behind me. I stopped and turned but I didn't stick my thumb up, I just waved. I felt like I was back in civilization again. The pickup pulled just past me and stopped. I walked up to the open window on the passenger side and as I looked in, an old man behind the steering wheel said, "Are you all right, son?"

I opened my mouth to speak, and nothing came out. I swallowed real hard, cleared my throat and tried again, "Yes sir, I'm doing a whole lot better than I look like I'm doing."

He asked where I was heading. I told him I was renting a room from a feller outside Florence on this road. "Are you the boy renting from Mr. Williams", he asked. I responded, "Yes sir, I am. Do you know Mr. Williams?"

"Shoot, I've know that old fart for nearly seventy years. Not a finer feller around these parts," he growled. "He's told me some about you...he thinks you are a fine boy. What the heck happened to you? Well, never mind - get in the truck and I'll take you home."

I paused and told him it would probably be better if I just hopped in the bed of his truck because I was wet and dirty.

"Damn boy, you don't need to do that. You aren't going to hurt the inside of this old truck any. Shoot, I've carried chickens and all kind of varmints right up here in the cab with me," he said as he turned and spit out the window.

I tried to knock some of the filth off of me and then crawled up into the cab trying to keep my pain to myself. As we pulled back out on the road he asked, "What in the world happened to you?" Then before I even opened my mouth he continued, "Nah, don't tell me, 'cause if you tell me, I'll probably tell old Williams, and if you want him to know what you been up to, you ought to be the one to tell him…By the way, my name is Bob Thomas, but you can call me Mr. Thomas, or you can just call me Thomas."

Mr. Thomas pretty much dominated the conversation for the rest of the trip, giving me a brief history of Florence and telling me how Mr. Williams had been responsible for it being a booming cotton town at one time. As we pulled into the driveway the sun was just starting to peek above the horizon.

"Well, looks like this is your lucky morning. Looks like old man Williams is sleeping in this morning. Maybe you'll have a chance to clean up and get a little sleep before you see him."

With that said, he reached across the seat and offered me his hand. As we shook hands he wished me luck, and told me when I got to feeling better to tell old Williams to bring me out to his place and we could do some fishing. I thanked him, slipped out of the seat, and closed the door. I then stuck my hand back inside, shook his hand and said thanks one more time. Mr. Thomas backed out of the driveway, waved and drove away. I never saw him again.

I walked around to the door to my room and noticed Jim's car was still there. I couldn't imagine where Jim might be, but resolved to find him as soon as I cleaned up and put on some decent clothes. As I walked into my room, to my astonishment, there on my bed asleep was Jim. As I walked over to him, he woke, threw back the cover and rolled out of bed saying, "Terry! Where in the hell have you been? What the hell happened to you? How did you get home? Man, you look like crap!"

I gave him an abbreviated version of my night, leaving out some of the more embarrassing parts, which was most of the story. He told me that they had come out of the restaurant and when they found that I wasn't in the car, they had searched every other restaurant, bar and business within walking distance looking for me. After hours of looking for me, they stopped a police car and explained that they had lost a friend. He went on to explain that the police officer made some calls on his radio, but advised that they had no information about me at that time. Jim said as they walked back to the car, the police officer pulled back up to them. He said he had just talked to another officer who stated he had just taken a man claiming to be Terry Beck and fitting his description, out to the edge of town, and was last seen walking toward Lampasas. He understood he was heading to Florence.

Jim said they rushed to their car and headed for Florence, hoping to find me along the way. He said they covered every inch of the way between Austin and the Florence cut off, and then all the way into Florence. I didn't go into all the details, but I told him that I may have taken a detour or two along the way. The way it sounded, I probably missed them while I was playing Davy Crockett out in the wilderness. Jim told his buddies to just leave him at my room. His plan was to call someone to open his shop, and then backtrack all the way to Austin to see if he could find me, as soon as he got a little rest.

I felt terrible, not just physically, but also because of what I had put Jim through. He was a real friend who, after knowing me for only six months, was genuinely concerned and obviously upset over the stunt I had pulled. I told him how sorry I was and how appreciative I was for his concerns and his efforts. I apologized repeatedly to the best of my diminished mental abilities and my semi-coherent verbal abilities. He said he was just glad that I was still alive, shook my hand, said he would see me later and left. Sadly, I never saw him again.

I took off what was left of my clothes, walked into the shower and there I stood for at least thirty minutes with my forehead against the cool tile, letting the clean cool water roll down the back of my neck. I walked out of the shower, dried off and checked my wounds to see if stitches would be needed. I called work and told the boss I wouldn't be in that day, but would be in to finish my last two days, then crashed on the bed. The next time I opened my eyes, it was dark and I was totally confused. I wasn't sure if it was the same day, but it didn't matter. I got up, used the bathroom and even though I was starving, got back in bed and slept some more.

I woke up again about three o'clock in the morning and just lay there, partly because there wasn't an inch on my body that didn't hurt, but mostly because I just didn't have the willpower, or maybe I should admit, I didn't have the mental strength to get out of bed. Finally, I got on my feet, walked over to the mirror and looked at my shredded body. I had lost what was then the love of my life but, my God, that was no reason to do that to myself. I was mad. I was ashamed. I was an idiot. How could anybody trust in me again? How could I ever trust myself again?

I guess I had been lucky. Other than the torture I put my body through, my only other loss was the loss of my billfold, about a hundred dollars in cash, my driver license, social security card and a few credit cards.

Then the day I was going to leave for home, my dad called. His first words were, "TD, are you all right?" He went on to say that he had received my billfold in the mail that morning from the Austin Police Department, and it scared him to death. I told him that I was fine, and that I had found out that I wasn't much of a drinker, but apparently I made one hell of a drunk. He told me the billfold had about a hundred dollars still in it and it looked like all my cards and stuff were still there. I told him that I would see him later in the day, that I would explain the mess to him, and that I loved him. He said, "Let's not tell your mom about this; she worries enough without stuff like this on her mind."

I couldn't believe I had been so lucky. So many things could have happened that didn't. What can I say? One thing, I know the ex-love of my life probably thought I would just sit around and mope, but by golly, I showed her.

Then there is this thing about my intelligence. While it is apparent that smart and I don't always get along very well, I really think that smarter and I may have a little thing going.

I am always mindful of the things that I have said that may have offended someone. You never know when you might want to offend them again.

I've Been Thinkin'

REVENGE OF THE MAILBOX

We moved into the house at 1409 Oakland Drive in 1953. I was four years old, but I can remember the pride my Dad had when we were able to move into our "own" house. One of the first things my Dad did was to put up a mailbox. To him that was like marking his territory or staking his claim, and he put his all into the project. Pop was a planner, even on the simplest of chores. He put in a lot of time planning and then installing our first mailbox. Concrete, four inch wooden post, white paint, red paint, black paint, stencils, brushes, nails, screws, post hole diggers, shovels and a store bought mailbox. He hand painted DON E. BECK and 1409 OAKLAND DR. on each side of the mailbox. No stick-on numbers or letters were used. It was a beautiful mailbox.

About a week after its installation, the mailman accidentally knocked the mailbox off its post when he struck it with the mirror on his truck. It was dented and the paint was scratched but Pop, being an accomplished body man, painstakingly made the necessary repairs. Then a few weeks later the mailbox was again knocked from its pedestal and again it was repaired and replaced. When approached about the incident, the mailman denied any guilt, but Pop was always a little suspicious.

Over the next several years the mailbox spent about as much time on the ground as it did on its post. Whether the mailman, us kids or those stopping by for a visit were the cause, it was difficult to keep our mail receptacle in place. Pop went back to the drawing board, and designed a mailbox that would fend off all attacks.

He simply welded four or five old automobile springs together to make the post or pedestal, then welded the mailbox on top of it. It did not have all the grace and beauty of the original box, but it has survived many a battle over the years. Pop always loved to tell the story of the mailman's first encounter with the spring mounted mailbox. My Dad made certain that he was home the first day the new box would be visited by the mailman. The mailman drove up to the box and quickly learned that it would take two hands to open the mailbox door, one to hold the box steady and the other to open the door. Then, apparently aggravated by the extra time (several seconds) involved in placing the mail, the mailman slammed the mailbox door. According to my Dad, "That mailbox almost beat the poor mailman to death before he could stop it from bouncing back and forth."

One thing that everybody in the vicinity of "The Mailbox" quickly learned: Whether checking the mail, mowing or just walking by, if you hit "The Mailbox", it was going to hit you back.

I've Been Thinkin'

THAT OLD MAN ON THE CORNER

I like thinking about the old days. I like thinking about happy days. I think about the sad times. I think about the bad times. When young, ninety percent of my thoughts were about my tomorrows. Today ninety percent of my thoughts drift back to my yesterdays. I'm not sure who will be sharing my tomorrows, but I thank God for those folks of yesterday, whose strength and wisdom guided me to where I stand today.

I've seen that old man on the corner, staring into what I had thought was the emptiness of lost days. I've seen that old man on the corner, dressed in yesterday's clothes, his skin weathered, grey hair blowing in the wind. I've seen that old man on the corner, alone and lonely, although I've never spoken to him to know for sure. He smiles as a handful of neighborhood kids ramble by in a quest for greener pastures. Then his gaze returns to the distant horizon as he pulls his watch from its pocket, winds it, and returns it to its pocket, never looking at the time.

Time passes, no matter what the speed. Memories are gathered, whether they be good or they be bad. Brown hair turns grey and the styles of today are noticed, but no longer important. The "whys and how comes" of life have mostly been figured out, and those that haven't were filed under 'not important'. Comfortable doesn't cover as many things as it used to, having more to do with the mind now, than with money.

I am content, I am happy, and I know who I am as I sit on my flagstone porch, comfortable with my little house on the corner.

The pictures line the walls, rest on the mantle and reside on shelves. Lives and memories frozen from that moment on. There are tears, sighs and smiles, but mostly smiles. Our life of today is made complete by all that was ours yesterday. So, clear the dust and show with pride all that was loved and all that was lost. They are more than just photographs, more than decorations; They are life's memories. They are us.

MOM

Going through all of Mom's memories is an experience that tests all emotions. I had known Mom all my life, yet it seems each day that I follow the thoughts and things that she has left behind, I find that I never knew it all. It seems that some of the greatest emotional reactions are stirred by the simplest of things.

I found a letter, postmarked February 24, 1948, that Mom wrote to her mother and father just three days after she and Dad were married. They had traveled from Blanket, Texas to Odessa, Texas because Dad had a couple of older brothers living in that area, and they had arranged employment for him.

That letter said in part:

> "Dearest Mom & Dad,
>
> We made it fine. We stayed Saturday night in San Angelo & got here about twelve thirty Sunday. We found a trailer house to stay in. It's about as big as our junk room, maybe a little longer. It has a bed, ice box, stove, cabinet with a sink, a dresser, a closet, a table with benches built on the wall, a door & six windows...

It is amazing that a life so filled with memories that go in every direction could begin so simply. There was the raising of five sons, helping Dad make ends meet when necessary, the illnesses, the education, the death of her own parents and the parents of my Dad, saying goodbye to each of us as we left home, welcoming the grandkids and then the great grandkids, helping Dad fight cancer to the end and finally the ten year battle she waged against her own cancer.

And it all began with "a bed, ice box, stove, cabinet with a sink, a dresser, a closet, a table with benches built on the wall, a door & six windows."

I've Been Thinkin'

A GOOD DAY, GOATS AND ALL

It was a good day, a really good day. Amber and I rolled out of bed early this morning, which in itself was something new and different. The plan was to travel to Mullin, visit with my Mom and Pop for a while, and place a Christmas wreath at their gravesite. We told Beaux Bo that we would be back in a little bit (not really sure how much he really understands about what we are doing or saying, but we usually lie to him just in case) and we were on our way. The sun was rising and the morning was crisp. Everything looked especially sharp, clear and beautiful, even the things we would normally look past.

To give an example of how good a mood I was in, as we were driving through Stephenville, Amber spotted a ladies clothing store that she thought might have a couple of gift items she had not been able to find around home and she asked if we could stop. I said yes, and as we pulled up to the front of the store, Amber said, "Oh no, it's going to be another twenty minutes before they open and I know you are in a hurry...let's go ahead and leave". Now get this: I actually said that I didn't mind, we could wait. The store opened on time, Amber found the items she had been looking for and was happy. I was still happy and a little bit amazed at myself.

We were on our way again, bound for Mullin, Texas. We took back roads the rest of the way. It was a beautiful trip. Amber has hearing loss and it is especially hard for her to hear and understand conversation with the distraction of the road and car noises. However, with trips like this, conversation is not necessary. We simply absorbed all that was there to see, and smiled an occasional acknowledgment to each other as we made our way.

We arrived at the cemetery and placed the wreath. All was quiet, with the exception of the hushed sound of the crisp cool wind. Nature had provided the perfect setting for a sharing of thoughts and feelings as we sat there with Mom and Pop. I was a child again as we spent a while remembering. It was good and I was still happy, in a different kind of way. We left without saying goodbye, but thinking more along the line of, "See you later".

From there we went to Goldthwaite and had lunch. The food was good, the people were kind. Everyone in the building knew each other. There was laughing, loud talking (the good kind) and a little cussing (the good kind, if that is possible). The setting just seemed to fit the mood that I had been in all day.

After eating, we had only one item left on the agenda: buy some pecans. We drove all the way across town (taking about two and a half minutes) and pulled up to the old warehouse next to the railroad tracks. As we started to the door, we noticed a sign that said they were closed because they were having their Christmas lunch for all their employees but they would all be back around 1:00PM. Amber asked if I wanted to just go on home. To her amazement, as well as mine, I told her we could wait. We drove around town for a while and killed four or five minutes and then found a beautiful little park. We parked at the park and made out for a few minutes. Not really, but when I told Amber that is what everyone would think, she sternly suggested that we leave.

When we arrived back at the pecan warehouse, they were open for business. We went in and bought a five pound bag of this year's shelled pecans. This may be a little hard to believe, but Amber bought something else before we left. It's not hard to believe that Amber bought something else, it's hard to believe what she bought. She bought an 8 ounce bottle of 'Nanny-Nanny-Boo-Boo' goat milk lotion made at Five Dish Goat Farm & Dairy, LLC, Mullin, Texas. This particular selection of 'Nanny-Nanny-Boo-Boo' (yep that's the brand name) goat milk lotion is coincidentally named "Amber". I could go on and on about this lotion, but I won't...

The trip home was as nice as the trip had been that morning, except we had pecans to eat. There are so many to be grateful to for such a wonderful day.

I've Been Thinkin'

I am thankful to Amber for her company and her loving understanding, to Mother Nature and all her brilliance, to Mom and Pop for my life, to the people of Goldthwaite who helped pass the day, and the goats for, well, you know.

Walked into the bedroom this morning and rather than admit to Amber that I had forgotten why I had walked there, I grabbed the vacuum, vacuumed the carpet, and cleaned the ceiling fan.

I don't think she suspected a thing...smoooooth!!

DIARY OF A PROJECT

I decided to have something nice done for Amber that I knew she would really like. Best of all, it would require very little work on my part. These are my notes from the project:

PART I

Had a guy come over and give me an estimate on constructing built-in cabinets and shelving that would cover one complete wall in the den and would look like a giant shadow box. Amber needs the space to display all the additional treasures from our parents' estates.

PART II

Cost was waaaaay more than I thought it would be, but decided to go ahead with the plan. Amber: Happy Birthday, Late Mother's Day, and Merry Christmas for a year or two. Now what does she mean by "We may have to rearrange some things to get ready for the cabinets..."?

PART III

Moved the king sized bed out of the front bed room, moved the entertainment center out of the living room to the den, and the entertainment center that was in the den to the living room, then moved a desk and queen sized bed into the front bedroom, and the king sized bed into the second bedroom. Then she said something I don't understand, "Of course this will all be temporary."

PART IV

Moved the bed and the 600 pound dresser in the back bedroom to four different walls, and also took all hanging items off all the walls. Apparently everything that is hanging on a wall in the house will have to be moved. Amber gave me the rest of the night off.

PART V

We took today off to be with family for the holiday weekend. We are waiting to hear from the cabinet maker as to when he is ready to start installing. Amber said when he calls is when the serious rearranging begins.

PART VI

Haven't heard anything from the cabinet dude yet. Haven't moved any furniture or taken anything down from the walls in nearly two days. I'm concerned! I've seen Amber doing some measuring and smiling as she walks from room to room. I've seen that smile before. Premedication may be the best plan.

PART VII

The cabinet dude called and is ready to begin installing the cabinets. Amber says all we have to do today is move all the furniture in the den up against the far wall and take all the hanging stuff off the walls. Amber has a way of making things SOUND easy.

PART VIII

It only took the cabinet dude about half a day to install the cabinets. I was hoping it would take days. It really looks nice. Big and empty, but nice. Then Amber said something rather disturbing, "Now's when the real work begins!"

PART IX

I have to be quick. Amber thinks I am in the bathroom. So far I've carried about 250 items into the room to place into the new cabinets, and Amber has used four of them. This may be worse than I thought. Oops, I hear Amber coming down the hall. I gotta go. Boy, that was a short honeymoon!!!

I've Been Thinkin'
PART X

Over the last couple of weeks, I have touched, moved, hung and re-hung everything in this house at least three times. I am tired, bruised, and have had my feelings hurt on several occasions, but it is done. It was all worth it just to see the satisfied smile on Amber's face as we sat together admiring her cabinets. Then, that's when she said, "This will be great - just think, we can rearrange the cabinets with every season and holiday: Fall, Spring, Summer, Christmas, Valentine's Day, Easter, Halloween, Thanksgiving..." Then she gave me a big ol' hug and kiss and said, "Thank you, sweetie!"

Chalk hopscotch squares and drawings on the driveway, more toys in the bathtub than the toy box, more clothes on the floor of the closet than hanging, stumped toes from toys left laying on the floor; don't be too anxious for these things to stop, because one day they will.

JUST ONE "DAY" FOR MOTHERS?

Mom, Mama, Mother, Ma - one of the most cherished titles ever received by a human being. Everybody was born to a mom and, if very fortunate, will have the opportunity to enjoy her company well into the later years of their love filled journey. I loved my mom and although I felt this emotion from the birth of my memory, the true impact of this love was not realized until she was no longer physically available. Even now, her intellect, her sacrifices, her strength and her all encompassing sense of humor sometimes overwhelm me in a storm of memories. As with any storm the intensity builds until I feel my heart would surely burst - then the calmness comes and with that, a smile.

It takes something really special to be a good mom. If we were to list all the qualifications of motherhood it would certainly appear to be an impossible task. Yet moms rise to the occasion every day, and they do it because of a natural strength and knowledge that has been embedded in their soul. Sadly, much of the time these daily feats of heroic ventures go unnoticed, and are taken for granted as routine chores.

We have a debt to pay. We have a debt to our wives who have unselfishly raised our children. We have an overdue debt to our moms or to their memory. The sum of this debt is incalculable, yet so easily paid. Love, recognition, affection and an occasional helping hand, while seldom asked for, will go a long way in paying this debt.

While weak in comparison to the many achievements of all the good moms, I want to offer my deepest appreciation for all that you have done and will continue to do. May your disappointments be few, your rewards be many, your wishes be fulfilled and most importantly, may the love you have invested be returned tenfold. You are all unbelievable women with unselfish hearts and an unbreakable spirit known as motherhood. Thank you one and all. Happy Mother's Day - Every day!

IF I COULD GO BACK

It is the child that still lives deep within even the oldest of us that allows thinking of, and sometimes even doing, things that the normal us would never do or think. This child within frees my mind to wander, not to worry about the bills, or the Cowboys or what the weather will be like two weeks from now, but to go beyond the possible and dream of what could be. This childlike curiosity of mine frees my mind from the grips of the acceptable and lets me reshape reality into something more comfortable.

I have become somewhat stoic when it comes to physical travel, but I have a busy mind when it comes to journeys within. My mind tends to travel back in time visiting the people, places and things that either affected my life or were somehow affected by me. Very seldom do I travel into the future, due to the lack of fuel for thought, or possibly a lack of imagination.

I often wonder, if I could go back, what would I change if I could? Then I argue: If you are content with your life now, why would you go back and change something that could change the good that you now have? So, the child within me establishes a new rule for going back: Anything you change, as long as it is for the better, will not change the happiness you now enjoy.

When I travel back to the early years of my life, I don't really take any exceptions, not because everything was perfect, but because the first ten years or so are pretty well protected by the "innocence of youth" clause. It's not until I reached the "you-should-know-better" stage of youth that I began to take exceptions to my life. One obvious change would be to not confuse love with infatuation. I wouldn't confuse want with need. I would think twice about sacrificing friendship for popularity. I would choose my friends based on who they were, rather than what others claimed they were.

While I am proud of my achievements, or at least my efforts, in sports, I think I would now learn more about the arts because the arts are a kinder companion to the older folks. I wouldn't always say "Me, too," when my heart was saying "Not me." I would appreciate the efforts and patience of my teachers and I would have told them so. I would know the difference between cute and smart ass and conduct myself accordingly.

I would have asked my mom and dad more questions. I would pay more attention to their words. I would have told mom I loved her every day and never, ever told her that I didn't love her anymore. I would hug and tell dad I loved him long before I found out he was dying. My little brothers and I would have gone fishing more together, and I would never lose touch with what was going on in their lives.

I wouldn't wait until I was sixty-four to tell everybody what I believed, how I felt and what I had on my mind.

Finally, I would travel back and find the person responsible for putting Daylight Savings Time in effect and talk him out of it.

I've Been Thinkin'

HE DOESN'T DANCE ANYMORE

I saw a man across the room who favored someone I used to know, someone I used to call friend. He sat there alone in the corner of the room, picking at the label on his bottle of beer. He looked older than he would be if he were my friend and he was alone, something I couldn't imagine if he was my old buddy. Not only would he always be in a crowd, he generally would be one of the leaders or a focal point of the group. No, I didn't think that was him, as he put out his cigarette in an ashtray already three fourths full of stale cigarette butts. He always thought of his body as a temple and was well aware he was a healthy, good looking man and did what he could to stay that way.

He stood and limped across the room to the jukebox. He was at least fifty pounds heavier than he should be, was bald, wore khaki pants and a wrinkled white shirt with green stripes. No, this couldn't be the long haired, athletic person who was always the first to wear 'the style' in clothes. As he slowly walked back to his table, I convinced myself that this was not my old friend. While he might be his older brother, it just wasn't him.

As I stood to leave, a song came on the jukebox that stopped me in my tracks. It was a Tommy James song, one of many of his songs that were a mainstay in every eight track player making the drag for years back home. I turned and looked at the old man in the corner as he hollered to the waitress, "Another beer!" and nodded his head to the beat of the rocking sweet music. Could it be a coincidence? Too many things said "Maybe not". I couldn't leave without knowing for sure.

I turned and walked slowly toward him, doubt still dominant in my mind. As I approached, still five or six steps from him, he looked up at me. For a moment there was only an empty stare, then a smile, a smile that lit up his face, a smile I had seen before. The doubt was gone. It was indeed him, my buddy, my old friend. As I approached with my hand extended, he stood, pushed my hand aside and wrapped both his arms around me. We stood in a man hug for a while before he finally said as he patted my back, "Terry Don, you old fart, it's so good to see you".

As we stepped back, I placed my hand on the back of his neck and told him how good it was to see him. He motioned to me to have a seat. As we sat, I heard him groan and saw his face twitch in pain. He asked if I wanted a beer and when I told him no, that I was just leaving, he ordered me one anyway.

We sat and talked of yesteryear with all its wonderful times and days of glory. As he talked, his face would light up and I could see the friend that had once been like a brother. We talked about all the good times and all the firsts that we had done together. We relived the dances, the parties, the games, the girls, the close calls and things nobody but us would ever know about. Several times he would refer to things he said we did, and laugh and slap the table. I laughed with him, even though the person he talked about was not me.

He asked me about my family and what I had been up to all these years. I told him of my loving family, my semi-successful career and my terrific retirement. As I spoke, he kept the smile on his face, but his eyes looked empty and his mind seemed to be elsewhere. I hesitantly asked him about his family and happenings. He looked down, picked up his beer, swirled the last couple of sips around in the bottle and said, "Been married four times, got two kids running around somewhere, and I sell stuff. By golly, I can sell just about anything". With that said, he chugged the last of his beer, raised it into the air and hollered, "Bring us another beer, Sweetheart!"

I motioned to the gal and told her to just bring one, as I needed to go. He reached over and slapped the back of my hand and said, "You don't have to go, Bro!" I paid for the beer and told him that I needed to get back home but we should get together again. We stood, hugged again and then I took his hand and asked, "Are you alright, Bro? Are you sure you are OK?"

He put his other hand on top of mine, cleared his throat and said, "I'm doing fine, old friend. I just don't dance any more".

Daylight Savings Time!! When it was first introduced, I can remember the trauma of having a date, wanting to go parking, but having to wait until after nine o'clock for it to get dark, and knowing my date had to be home by ten.

Or was it me that had to be home by ten?

I've Been Thinkin'

WHATEVER I WANT

―――◆―――

I can remember way back when I was on the short side of four feet tall, going to school for what seemed like an eternity. Then I'd get out for the summer for ninety days and it seemed like a week. I can remember thinking, "I can't wait until I no longer have to go to school and I can do whatever I want". I remember peddling around and around and around the block on my Western Flyer bicycle with strips of cardboard attached to the fender brace striking the spokes, and how that clattering noise seemed to make me go faster. I remember thinking, "I can't wait until I'm old enough to drive a car and go where ever I so desire, whenever I want, even if it is ten miles away."

Then there were the "can't win for losing" days when I was grounded for a week because my younger brothers couldn't keep their mouths shut. I couldn't wait until I could get away from my brothers and do what I wanted without worrying about them telling on me and getting in the way. There were all the times that I asked Mom and Dad if I could go somewhere neat because all, and I mean every single one, of my friends were going and they told me no. They never would understand. It sure would be great when I could make my own decisions without having to talk to Mom and Dad.

I remember working at Dad's shop in the summer and on weekends to make a little spending money, and still have to ask for a little more when Mom would take us to the movie. My thoughts are still clear, "I can't wait until I get a real job so I can buy all kinds of stuff any time I want". I can still remember Friday nights with the sound of the bands playing, the smell of popcorn, beautiful girls and their huge mum corsages with ribbons and bells galore, and then the thrill of seeing the hometown football team charge onto the field. I remember thinking,

One of these days that will be me. I'll be a star and get a scholarship to whereever I want to go."

There were so many times in the middle part of my life when I dreamed of the time when I would no longer have to work, the kids would be gone and I could do all the things I have always wanted to do. I could fish, hunt, travel, party, or, if I wanted, I could do absolutely nothing. It would be nice to be the master of my life, owing nothing to a soul, obligated to no one but me, always traveling light with nobody's baggage but my own.

The years passed at an amazing speed. Memories have amassed, some good, some bad, some blurred. Despite my efforts, as well as an occasional lack thereof, I have made it to that point in my life that I have always been striving for. I am financially stable, basically healthy, have nothing but time, and I'm old. I can do what I want to do. I can think about riding my bicycle with streamers, clappers and friends. I can think about my brothers and how I miss seeing them more. And then there is Mom and there is Dad…how I wish you were still here to give advice, laugh with, hold and love.

Yes, I can do whatever I want to whenever I want. It turns out that's not as much as I had always thought it would be. I have Amber, Beaux Bo, family, friends and mountains of memories and they make me the master of my soul with a heart obligated to all that have traveled with me.

STILL ALIVE & KICKIN'

If I owned a newspaper, I think I would have a Still Alive & Kickin' page. I would have it preceding or following the Obituary page…probably following. Folks would pay the same as they do for obits, so much per line or so much per word. You could put a new photo, an old photo, or both and any other information you would feel comfortable seeing in print.

The main thing would be to not only show off that you're still alive, but also the family you so proudly share that life with. I can hear it now as someone opens up the paper and says, "I'll be damned, ol' Terry Beck is still alive. Why, I haven't thought of him in years. And looky here, he finally got a woman to hang around long enough to get married. I guess she must have straightened his act up, or he wouldn't still be around. I wonder if he remembers that $200 he owes me".

A Gathering of Words

Time passes, opinions change, appearances wane, our pace slows. Thoughts come more slowly, but are more meaningful. Eyes fail, yet we see more clearly. Time still passes. In years past, days seemed like weeks, but now weeks seem like days.

Time still passes, but now its value is clear.

I've Been Thinkin'

OUR HALL TREE

Today we cleaned up and found a spot to display an antique hall tree well over a hundred years old. We made a trip to Mom's house and brought back several items, including the hall tree. They had been treasures to my folks. Some of them had been treasures of their folks, as well. Some of the items probably have monetary value of some sort. Some are only treasures of the heart.

We worked about half the day on the old hall tree trying to clean the dust of years past from its nooks and crannies. Now clean, the old hall tree still displays the scars of its past, but still stands with a certain air of majesty. After finishing the superficial cleansing, I stepped back to inspect the finished product. What happened to me then was very un-Terry-like.

I stared into the mirror for the first time with thought. As I peered into the stained and aged glass at my face, I suddenly realized I was in the presence of more than an old piece of furniture. My normally simple mind began to swirl with thoughts and questions. How many others had looked at the reflection of their face in that mirror? What were their thoughts at that moment? What emotion was being reflected as they stood before the mirrored hall tree?

I could see my great grandma checking her hat to make sure it sat just right before walking out the door on her way to church. I could see Papa Dan staring into the mirror as he hung his hat on the peg, possibly trying to figure how to tell Mama May Delle that he was going fox hunting with Jesse Marlin. I saw Pop looking into the mirror adjusting his uniform before telling Mom good-bye as he prepared to go overseas. I saw Mom looking into the mirror with a smile as she paused for only a moment before she continued the chores necessary when raising five boys

The people that passed before that old hall tree were an important part of my becoming who I am today. I hope to preserve it for those that follow, in hopes that they too will look into its reflective window and have fond thoughts of those of us who have stood before it, seeing more than just our own reflection.

I've Been Thinkin'

THE BACK PORCH

The back porch has been and still is one of the most meaningful places in my life. There are those who have beautiful covered patios that are great for entertaining, or to just stand there and look at. A back porch is an emotional place, a place to gather your thoughts or to clear your mind completely. When I built this house over twenty years ago and then remodeled the back portion of the house about ten years ago, the builder kept making references to the nice sunroom and covered patio that I was going to have when he finished. I was a little taken aback at the idea of a covered patio instead of a back porch.

A few months after the remodeling was completed I began to feel like maybe the builder was wrong about the patio. It felt more like a back porch to me. Then one day in May it was confirmed. I did indeed have a back porch. My parents came to visit, which was especially meaningful because my Dad was fighting cancer, and we knew he only had a few months left on this earth. When they arrived, Dad walked into the house looking really tired after the trip. He commented on how good the house looked, shook my hand, hugged Amber and walked straight out the back door and pulled up a chair and had a seat. I followed him outside and had a seat next to him. He leaned back, crossed his legs, looked around for a minute or so and then said, "You've got a really nice back porch, TD. I like it". That's when I knew I had me a back porch.

Sitting on the back porch always makes my day better. It makes the bad things seem not quite as bad. When I'm sitting there the aches and pains in my old joints fade, and I am able to think without all the distractions of the body and the battles of the soul. My mind floats, mostly back to younger times when the kids were running around in the back yard laughing and hollering for me to watch as they showed me how they had learned to cartwheel, or flip, or twirl a baton and I would smile. I sit and watch the dog chase and push his ball around in the yard with his nose and I laugh and clap at a job "well done, Beaux Bo".

There are times I sit on my back porch and watch the wind blow the leaves of the trees and feel it blow across my face as the stress and worries trapped within me are set free. I think back to Dad sitting on our little back porch back home, watching me and my brothers play ball and hollering instructions on how to be better and how to beat the best. I remember Mom and Dad finally remodeling the old house and adding on more rooms. When it was finished, Mom informed Dad that he would no longer be allowed to smoke inside the house. Dad called the builder they had used and informed him that he was not finished. The builder was given instructions to build a huge screened in back porch and he built a nice one. Dad was proud of his back porch.

As I sit here on my back porch, I can see Dad sitting in his old chair listening to his old AM radio, pulling for his Brownwood Lions, hollering instructions as if the coach could actually hear him, as the cool night breeze cleared the cigarette smoke from his back porch. I can remember sitting with Dad, sharpening our knives and talking about things that needed talking about, and at times not talking at all. I think back to the conversations we had on that porch the last few weeks when he told me everything was going to be alright, to keep an eye on Mom and the brothers... and I remember hugging him and telling him that I loved him and he said he loved me. Although I always knew Dad loved me and I hoped he knew I loved him, that evening on Dad's back porch was the first time I ever said it to him or he to me.

So, I've got a back porch even though some might say it looks like a patio. To find out what you have just simply go out back, either by yourself or with someone you love, sit down, take a deep breath to clear your mind and see if you can dream. See if you can see and hear things that you've never noticed before. Clear your mind and let your soul bask in the memories of all that has been good. If you are able to accomplish all these things or more, there is a good chance that goodness itself is yours, and it resides on your back porch.

I've Been Thinkin'

Pop sitting on his little back porch while my youngest daughter (then 7 years old, now 34) shows him an injury to her leg. A short time later pop built his screened in porch in the same location.

Wasting? Is that a part of getting older? Is being older construed as being useless? The years have left their mark. They have also instilled their wisdom. We have not been consumed by age, we have been strengthened by the experience of living. Wasting? I think not.

TRANSITIONS

There is a huge red oak tree with thousands and thousands of leaves. The leaves are in transition from green to orange and red and then finally to brown. They will finally lose their battle and fall to the ground and the wind will shuffle and carry them to all sorts of places.

As for me, I have made a pact, I will check the tree daily until all the leaves have fallen but one. I would like to witness the last leaf on this mighty tree. If possible, I would like to see it fall as I wonder what gave that leaf the strength to stay when all others had gone. How was it determined that it would be the last?

And then, after it has fallen, it will be as all the other leaves to everyone but me. I will pick it up and hold it for a while and try to understand, and then simply give it to the wind and let nature fulfill its wonderful end.

If ignorance is bliss, it seems to me that there should be more happy people out and about. I know I am one happy camper.

I've Been Thinkin'

'SPLAIN SOMETHIN' TO ME

Okay, I've been around for nearly sixty-four years. Sure, there are a few things I can't remember, like the first two or three years of my life, a few blank spots in the late 1960s and early 1970s and then there are the times I walk into a room and forget the reason why.

But I can remember gasoline selling for nineteen or twenty cents a gallon. I've sat back over the last several years waiting for someone to explain a few things that I apparently don't understand about economics. I guess either everybody else is sitting back waiting for someone to explain it, or everybody but me already knows the answers.

Well, I'm getting tired of waiting, so I'm going to ask! Several months ago, gas was selling for almost four dollars a gallon. Then, very slowly, gas started coming down, a penny one day, about a week later another penny and over several months (coming down a penny here and there) gas finally got down to less than two dollars a gallon and because our memories are so bad, we were happy paying two dollars a gallon. Then whamo - gas jumped up ten cents in one day, then another dime in a few days. As a matter of fact, yesterday gas was $3.18 and today it is $3.29 a gallon. How come? Why does it take months to come down a penny at a time, but jumps up ten cents a whack or more?

So, while I'm showing my ignorance, here's something else I don't understand. I bought gas in Burleson for $3.03 a gallon for a trip to San Angelo a while back. As I went through Cresson, about fifteen miles away, gas was $3.24. Then as I went through Granbury, forty-five miles away, gas was $3.03 on one side of town and $3.25 on the other side of town. Brownwood's gas was $3.13 to $3.14 and finally, when I arrived in San Angelo, it was $3.24 a gallon. How come? There was no great desert between these locations, no oceans, the weather was all about the same and the gasoline brands were all the same. Why such a big difference in cost?

Then there are the reasons for gas to go up. Here comes a hurricane. Oops - an oil spill. Brrr - really cold weather or really hot weather. Of course, wars in the middle east, and then there is the dreaded demands of vacations. Now it's to the point these things don't even have to happen for gas to go up. Gas can now go up if there might be a hurricane, or if there's a threat of an uprising, or a chance this could be a cold winter. How come? Haven't there always been hurricanes, cold/hot weather and vacations? I'm not much of a businessman, but when planning my cost/profit part of my business, I'm going to figure in all the possibilities from the beginning and make allowances, not simply react every time there is an occurrence and look for someone else to pay off my shortcomings.

Finally, with all their problems, the hurricanes, wars, spills, Mother Nature and the shortages, how come they are making more profit now than they ever have (and I'm not real sure who "they" are). If they are that good, maybe they should be running our government...or are they already doing it?

Hell, I'm goin' to bed!!

I've Been Thinkin'

NO GOOD DEED GOES UNPUNISHED

My workout/racquetball buddy and close friend of thirty years sold his house and is moving to Caldwell, Texas with his wife to retire. At least that's what he hopes. I have made many offers of assistance to him and his wife as they begin the dreaded moving ordeal. I told him that I had moving boxes of several sizes stored in my attic that I will never need and that he was welcome to use them.

Last night he called me and said that he would like to take me up on the moving box offer. I told him that he was welcome to them and he said he would be right over. I moved a vehicle out of the garage so that we would have access to the attic. He arrived shortly and I motioned for him to back into the driveway and guided him back until about half of his pickup truck was inside the garage. It was a cold and rainy night and we needed the protection of the garage to load the boxes. He had backed into the garage to where the driver's side door was extremely close to the hedges that line that side of the house. After much effort he was able to squeeze his not so petite body out of the truck.

I told him that I would go up into the attic and he could go up the steps to the opening and I would bring the boxes to him. He could just drop them to the garage floor. Off we went, feeling confident about our simple objective. (Now as I tell this story, remember this is two 60-year-old men just doing a simple chore.) I worked my way over to where the disassembled boxes were stored. I had placed those boxes there twenty-one years ago. I had placed them in the far reaches of the attic where there was no flooring and there were cable wires, electrical wires, rafters, roofing nails penetrating through the roof and only a few feet of clearance.

It was necessary for me to contort my not so supple body into all sorts of positions in order to get to the boxes. (I was thirty-eight years old when I placed the boxes in this out-of-the-way location.) Anyway, as I was snaking my way to the boxes I began to experience what would turn out to be a series of cramps. Some in my legs, some in my arms and some in my back. You can't imagine the panic that poured over me when I realized that there was not enough room to stretch out and offer relief to the cramps, not to mention what the nails sticking through the roof were doing to me.

I could give more details, but I think you probably get the idea. We finally accomplished our mission. As I climbed down from the attic, I looked as if I had disturbed a mama bear, torn clothes and all. We loaded the boxes in the back portion of the truck cab and my buddy once again squeezed between the shrubs and his truck to get into the driver's side door, pressing the truck door against the shrubs that were covered in Christmas lights. It is necessary at this point to point out that these Christmas lights were the net type with each section about two feet high and six feet long. Each section has about one hundred small white lights on it, and I had four sections plugged together to cover the row of shrubs.

As he finally got into the truck, I stood there in the garage relieved that this ordeal was over. I waved as my buddy slowly pulled out of the garage and headed down the driveway. I heard a strange noise and then I realized that he was pulling my Christmas lights off the shrubs. I began to holler and whistle trying to get him to stop. He stopped just as his truck was pulling out on the street. Apparently he had closed his door on some of the decoration wiring. All four sections had been pulled from the shrubs and now trailed down the driveway. It was still a cold rain falling, so I just pulled the lights back to the garage to check the next day, and told my concerned buddy not to worry about it.

I walked into the house and past my wife. She looked at me with concerned eyes, and I could tell she wanted to say something but didn't. Thank goodness. I had been relaxing in my easy chair for about twenty minutes when my cell phone rang. It was my old buddy. He was out of breath but I understood him to say that he was at Home Depot and that he couldn't find his billfold and he thought that he might have lost it at my house. Concerned, I jumped up, grabbed a flashlight and ran outside without taking time to put on a jacket. I looked in and around the shrubs, along the driveway and even out in the street. I pulled the car back out of the garage and looked there. I went back up in the attic. Still no billfold.

I was back out in the cold rain looking along the driveway when my cell phone rang. It was my buddy. He said that he had some good news. He had called his wife and she had found his wallet in the jeans that he had changed out of just before leaving. He said that he was sorry for any trouble that he had caused. As I stood there shivering with the cold rain running down my nose I told him that it was no trouble at all; I was just glad that he found his wallet

Always happy to help a friend…

The other day I just listened to Taps and cried. A while back, a friend told me that his trusty little dog and longtime companion had died, and I got a lump in my throat and couldn't talk. When I watch commercials about abused animals, I become angry and get tears in my eyes. I think a lot about those that are gone and how much I miss and need their company.

Emotions...a long time coming.

I've Been Thinkin'

HEY MOM, HEY POP – IT'S ME

———◆———

Well howdy Mom, hey Pop -just thought I'd share a few thoughts with you tonight. I know you know all this stuff, but it feels better if I go ahead and tell you any way. I think about y'all just about every day, most times, several times a day. Most all my thoughts are good ones, but every once in a while a not so good a thought comes along... mostly stuff that I did wrong or could have done better that I know disappointed you. Almost every day I either see something, hear something or read something that reminds me of you and the things y'all did for me. Sometimes it makes me a little sad that you aren't with us anymore, but then I get to thinking that's kind of selfish because I know your work is done down here and you are in a much better place now. But... I still miss y'all a bunch.

I know you would be proud of Shanon and Shaye, and the grandkids (your great-grandkids) Emily, Cole and Abbie. I guess it still bothers me a little because y'all didn't get to spend more time with them, especially the grandkids. But I can see a little of me in them and I guess that means there's some of y'all in them, too, and that's good. Every once in a while we all sit around and look at all your old pictures and mementos. They ask a hundred questions every time, but I don't mind because it helps me remember. It also makes me proud that they want to know more about you and when they ask if I still miss you, I say, "Always."

Pop, I see what you meant about the retired life. It is the greatest thing since sliced bread. I just wish you could have stayed around a little longer so we could have enjoyed a little of it together. You remember how you always wanted a place with a pond? Well, I don't have a pond like you wanted, but I did build me a creek, and I think you would like it. I sit out by The Creek a lot and think about our talks out on the back porch, and how much I miss them. Oh yeah, I hope you've seen The Rock and don't mind that I moved it from Brownwood to here. I guarantee it is well taken care of. I touch it almost every day and remember.

Mom, Amber has sure done a great job sharing all the things that were a part of you and of Mama Mae Delle. She really does a wonderful job and has such a good feel for how to display so many precious memories. I know we always made fun of how you saved everything and wouldn't throw things away, but now those things are a blessing and I thank you. I miss all our phone conversations, especially our Sunday night calls. It's hard to keep up with all the Brownwood gossip without our calls, but there's plenty of gossip up here to keep me busy. I do catch myself thinking about calling you on some Sundays and it is a little sad, but then I think of all the gossip you could tell me now if you could, and that helps.

Well, I've been doing the best I can, trying to stay happy and keep everybody else happy, too. Sometimes that's harder work than you would think it should be, but I know y'all know that. I hope you don't mind, but there are a lot of times when I use the stories and tales you told me to get a point across, and they are still as effective as always. One thing that kind of bothers me a little is that I wish I had asked more questions about some of the kinfolks, about your younger days and just things in general. There is hardly a day that goes by that I don't run across a question or two that I sure wish I could ask you, and it bothers me that I will never be able to.

Well, I guess you've noticed our handy work out at Mullin. We try to keep things spruced up according to the season and make sure that things are as good as they can be. Amber has already bought some really pretty Christmas decorations, so I guess we'll be heading back that way sometime after Thanksgiving and fix things up. Although I talk to you all the time, our talks among the monument stones always seem special. It's like we are all together again with Mama Mae Delle, Papa Dan, Tate, La Juana and all the other cherished family members.

It's getting late and I guess I'd better go. It is my hope that the things we do and the things we say make you proud. I am certainly proud of who you are to us and all that you made happen so that we could be who we are today. I miss you...I will love you always...Good night.

I've Been Thinkin'

TO RUN AND PLAY AGAIN

―――――◆―――――

I sit in a sterile room, free of color and warmth, where minutes seem more like hours, and hours can be torturous. Fresh air is but a memory and the weather matters not as I sit with Danny, my brother and friend, as he lies tangled in yards of tubes and wires hooked to noise making monitors and machines. He lies there, his tired body gripped and controlled by various "marvels" of medicine, and as I look at a face that should be more recognizable, I wonder if at least his soul is still his to control. I stand and walk to his side. As I stand looking down on him my mind drifts back to his magical days of glory, when his potential and natural abilities were boundless, and a confident smile was his dominant pose. Sadly, he doesn't run and play anymore.

He is on a quest for better health as the masters of medicine work their miracles trying to reverse the effects of age, heredity and the demons of his past. I stand and listen to his labored breaths and I wish this was over, that all was as it once had been, and we were all home surrounded by family and friends. As I reach over, place my hand on his head and smooth his tousled hair, his eyes open, and for a moment he looks lost and confused. Slowly, his eyes appear to focus and a slight grin emerges on his face as I say, "Welcome back, Bro!"

He becomes frustrated as he tries to speak. I quickly pull my chair next to his bed and begin to talk, hoping to calm him and let him know everything is okay and he isn't alone. I talk about everything and nothing. I speak about our childhood, Mom, Dad, and brothers Chris, Pat and Steve. His eyes never leave me as I go on about our romping and stomping through the old neighborhood. Slowly, his eyes close and he is asleep again.

I lean back, rub my old sore knee and sigh. I close my eyes and continue my thoughts of a younger day, and all that was ours to enjoy and share. Memories can be a wonderful thing. Memories can lift our souls, and let us run, and just for a moment, let us play again.

I've Been Thinkin'

ME AND THE RIFLEMAN

The water main just outside our house broke this morning, so we were without water all day. This afternoon I took a nap. I dreamed I was in the desert with the Rifleman and his son Mark gathering salt to take home, when our horses ran off with the wagon and water barrel. We were so thirsty, and I looked over and there was Amber drinking bottled water. I asked where she got it, and she said, "Out of the refrigerator". That's when Lucas (The Rifleman) asked "What's a refrigerator?"

About that time, Beaux Bo started digging in the sand near some rocks. All of a sudden, Bud Light came bubbling out of the ground. That's when Mark hollered, "Paw! Paw! Do you want me to get the peanuts?"

Lucas said, "OK son, remember I love you and remember what I have always taught you: Save a Horse, Ride a Cowboy is just a song."

About that time, Lucas started rapid firing his rifle at hundreds of buzzards that were trying to drink our Bud Light. That's when I woke up to the sound of Amber in the kitchen, beating the heck out of some steaks to tenderize them for dinner tonight.

I guess the Rifleman and Mark will have to get their own supper.

I don't guess Amber and I have the perfect marriage, but it is close enough to perfect for me. One reason that we do so well together is that we keep things simple. Our basic philosophy is "If you're OK, I'm OK". If we know that to be a fact, we just keep doing what we've been doing.

I've Been Thinkin'

DON'T KNOW HOW WE DID IT

I was just thinking back, trying to figure out how two people who had never raised children before could have managed to raise two girls, in my biased opinion, into well above-average, intelligent, beautiful, and kind women and mothers. Even though there may have been a hiccup or two in the raising process, I think we did an above adequate job.

I remember when Shanon, our oldest, was about four years old. I was walking by her bedroom door and stopped to watch her play. She was cooking away with her play kitchen all set up just like Mom's. She was humming and stirring and mixing stuff when she accidentally knocked a container off the cabinet and onto the floor. "Well crap," she said.

Shocked by the language coming out of her four year old mouth, I stepped into the room and shouted, probably louder than I should have, "What did you say?"

She looked at me, and with complete innocence repeated the word. I asked where she had heard that word. She said, "Momma always says that when she spills stuff in the kitchen."

I have never heard Amber say over a half dozen minimally profane words in the hundred years that I have known her. However, I don't hang out in the kitchen that much. I didn't feel it was necessary to send Shanon or her mother to Profaners Anonymous.

Then there was the time we were driving downtown when I looked in the rear view mirror only to see Shanon, again, happily waving her middle finger at cars as they passed. I pulled the car over and asked my still four year old daughter who she had ever seen do that. She informed me that was the way her two aunts, who were still in high school, always waved to their friends. Profane Gesturers Anonymous?

Then there was Shaye, my younger daughter. Shaye was always getting into something and wasn't very good at hiding it. I could find something that was newly broken, approach her holding it in my hand and ask her why she had broken it. She would nearly always confess, then ask how I knew it was her that had broken it. I would always say "A little birdie told me."

That's the way it went. She would do something wrong and I would bluff her into confessing. When asked how I had known, I always told her the little birdie had told me. One day, as I was sitting in my easy chair, Shaye walked over, climbed into my lap, looked at me with as serious a look as a young child could muster and asked "Daddy, just exactly what does this little bird look like?"

I'm not exactly sure when she finally grew out of her bird phobia, but for a long time if there were birds within sight, Shaye was on her best behavior.

Maybe they grew up to be such fine ladies in spite of our efforts. However, if it is acceptable with them, I would like to feel that we did make a difference. I can say, without hesitation, that Shanon, Shaye and Amber, my sweet wife, have made all the difference to me.

I've Been Thinkin'

IN A HEARTBEAT

On Sunday, December 17, 2000, I woke up and started piddling around the house. I had been called out to work for a couple of hours that night, but was feeling good and full of energy. I should have gone to church, but didn't. We ate lunch and after watching part of a football game, I called my old buddy, Ronnie, and asked if he wanted to go work out for awhile. As usual, he was ready to go, so I drove by, picked him up and we were off to the fitness center. Unless work interfered, Ronnie and I worked out with weights on Sunday, Tuesday and Thursday, and played racquetball on Monday, Wednesday and Friday.

We had a good workout. We lifted weights for about 1 1/2 hours, then rode the stationary bicycle for another thirty minutes. As we were changing clothes in the dressing room, I felt a little discomfort in the middle of my chest. It felt a lot like the feeling you get when you go outside when it is really cold and do some heavy work and after breathing in the cold air you get a kind of burning feeling in your chest. I really didn't think much about it. As we pulled up to Ronnie's house, he looked over at me and said that I was looking a little pale. He asked if I was feeling alright and I assured him that I was fine. I told him I felt like I might have a little congestion starting up in my chest, but that I was probably just getting a chest cold.

After getting home, I watched the end of another football game on TV, ate a good supper, watched a little more TV with Amber, and went to bed at my usual 9:00 PM. I awoke the next morning at 4:00 AM, ate my usual breakfast, read the paper, and was off to work a little before 6:00 AM, feeling great. I worked for eight or nine hours, went home, changed into my workout clothes, and met Ronnie at the fitness center for our usual day of racquetball. I'd had a good day and was feeling like I was going to kick some butt on the racquetball court.

There were four of us, as I recall, playing doubles racquetball. About ten to fifteen minutes into the game, I began having the same sensation in the middle of my chest that I had felt the day before. As I continued playing, the sensation began to worsen and my energy level began to fall. I finally told my fellow players that I thought I was feeling the effects of a cold, and I thought I would bow out, but that they should continue playing. Ronnie again looked at me and said that I didn't look good and asked if I was going to be all right. I assured him that I was going to be fine, and that I would call him later.

As I sat in the dressing room, I began to sweat profusely. I began to feel nauseous. The pain in my chest became more severe and I began to have pain in my shoulders and arms. For some reason, all I was thinking was that I needed to get away from all these people if I was going to be sick. I grabbed my bag and began the 200 yard walk to my truck. Every step that I took was becoming more of a chore. As I reached my truck it was obvious that I needed medical help.

The fitness center is part of the Huguley Hospital campus so the ER was not but a quarter of a mile from where I was sitting. There were thousands of things running through my mind: my wife Amber, the kids...What was I going to do? I knew I needed to let someone know where I was heading. About that time I saw a familiar face walking by. I shouted to him to please go in and tell Ronnie that I was heading to the ER and that I was feeling pretty bad. I would let him call Amber after we knew more about what was happening.

I had become so ill that I didn't even try to back out of the parking space, I just pulled my truck over the curb and drove through the grass to get to the road to the ER. There was one parking space left right in front of the ER entrance. I pulled in and walked into the ER where there were four or five people standing in line at the admittance desk. I can remember thinking that I might not make it. I must have looked pretty pitiful, because as soon as I walked up to the line of people, a nurse standing behind the desk came running around the corner, grabbed a wheelchair and rolled me into a room. Within seconds it seems like there were a dozen people buzzing around me hooking me up to stuff, putting pills by the dozen in my mouth and asking me hundreds of questions.

I began to have difficulty breathing. The pain in my chest increased by the minute. Through the commotion, I looked up and saw Ronnie standing at the foot of the bed. I remember asking him to please call Amber, thinking it might be best not to wait any longer. I can remember the pain shooting down my arms and my chest felt as though there was an elephant sitting on it. Then my hands started tingling and going numb. Sweat was rolling off my body and into my eyes. Things started getting a little fuzzy as they increased the morphine in my system. I remember saying I felt nauseous and a nurse placed what looked like a banana split bowl on my chest. Then I heard a familiar voice say, "I got you covered, Bro!" and there was Ronnie standing next to me holding a trash can. Ronnie then leaned over and told me to hang on, that Amber was on her way.

I remember waking from what I thought was sleep and then realizing that this was real. It had not been a dream, and the fear I felt was like nothing I had felt before. I remember calling out and asking "Where is my wife, where is Amber?" Then I heard her sweet voice and felt the touch of her hand and I felt better. I wasn't alone.

I really only remember bits and pieces of the next few hours. I know the fear that I had felt earlier had gone. I can remember them moving me to the intensive care unit. I can remember as they were picking me up to place me into the new bed, I felt a pain that was like an ice pick going through my heart and the chaos began again. I remember someone asking, "How much morphine has he had?", and then saying, "Give him more."

Although almost like a dream, I can remember people standing around the bed holding hands and praying. I can remember my family -- Amber, Shanon and Shaye and wanting to tell them everything would be ok, but I couldn't speak. I remember opening my eyes and seeing people with helmets standing around the bed and one leaning down and telling me that he understood that I needed to get to another hospital that was fifteen miles away real quick, and that they were the people who could do that. I can remember the cool breeze hitting my face as they loaded me into a helicopter.

I don't remember anything else until I woke up in the operating room and started to move. Several people grabbed me and hollered, "Don't move!" I guess I wasn't supposed to wake up at that particular moment. They performed a heart catheterization, performed an angioplasty, and placed a stent. The next day the Cardiologist told me that I was a very lucky man in that I had the heart attack so near to the ER. He also told me that the good folks at the smaller, less equipped Huguley Hospital had saved my life. He told me if I had been ten minutes farther away, or if the ER professionals hadn't acted as rapidly and efficiently as they had, I would never have made it to him. He went on to say that due to the initial ER treatment he saw absolutely no permanent heart damage or scarring.

I went home from the hospital Christmas Eve. I am a lucky man. I am so very thankful for the wonderfully gifted people who were there in my time of need, and that includes my wonderful family, and of course my bud, Ronnie.

My reason for sharing this story is not to provide entertainment, but to share something that I would never want to go through again. Nor would I want family or friends to be faced with such a horrific event.

Did you know, according to some medical studies, if you can't walk a quarter mile in less than five minutes, you are twenty-five percent more likely to die in the next six years than if you can? Or that if we eliminated all cancer in the United States, our average life expectancy would increase by only three years?

So, listen to your body. Don't deny what it is trying to tell you. Take care of your health. If I had listened to my body on December 17, 2000, I would not have gone through the agony of December 18, 2000. If you are younger, older, male or female, please take care of yourself. You are important to your family. You are important to your friends. You are important to me.

Your future is always a heartbeat away.

I've Been Thinkin'

WE ALL DRANK BROWNWOOD WATER AND DIDN'T TURN OUT SO BAD

Well, I headed out westbound for Brownwood, Texas this weekend and ended up somewhere between 1966 and 1968. It was my class of '67' forty-fifth reunion with good friends from the adjacent classes of '66' and '68' mixed in to add to the enjoyment. As we walked up to open door of the Morelock Barn we could see the silhouettes of dozens of folks who, at first glance, were not readily recognized, but there was no mistake about the music that was spilling out the door. It was 1967 all the way.

I could feel the excitement building in anticipation of being with many of the folks that had been a credible part of shaping who I am and the reason why I do the things I do the way I do them. We had grown up drinking the same water, riding down the same streets and sharing the air of champions in one of the finest and biggest little towns around.

As we walked through the doors there were about fifteen seconds of uneasiness and then someone hollered, "Hey, Terry Beck! How in the hell are you doing, you old fart?" From that point on there was nothing but good times and talking and a lot of fast talking. After all, we had forty-five years worth of stuff to talk about, not to mention the ten or twelve years prior to that. Then there was the hugging. You know, them Brownwood gals are still some of the finest huggers around. The guys, not so much good man huggers. Really, though, it was the first time most of us guys had hugged each other, 'cause guys didn't hug guys back in 1967.

Initially, I looked at my friends and fellow classmates, noticing all the changes and the reshaping they had gone through, but as we talked on into the night, laughed, relived and revived the souls of old, I was once again talking to the teenage faces and personalities that I knew and appreciated back in the springtime of our lives. I talked to them all and would love to list all their names. I think I can, but I won't; if I were to leave out a name it would be a shame because I loved seeing them all and they all had so much to do with recharging my old soul.

Even with the distance that time had put between us, we all still had so much in common. I'll have to admit a little feeling of disappointment when I listened to all that they had done and think, "How could you have done all that without me. We were supposed to do all that together." But, we had all gone our separate ways, learned new things, met new people and learned to drink water of a different land. I did learn that time, money, hardships, distances and doing all the things it takes to live and love today hadn't taken away the things we had in common and the bond that will forever be ours.

I've Been Thinkin'

JUST A SIMPLE NIGHT

Most times we sit in our favorite chairs, side by side, separated by an end table and a lamp, facing the television and, depending on whose time it is, holding Beaux Bo. When we talk, we don't look at each other because the lamp is in the way. We have our favorite shows we usually record so we don't have to watch the commercials, and we can go potty when we want and not at the mercy of live TV programming. We enjoy watching a variety of shows and movies, but funny stuff is our favorite. I love listening to her laugh or sometimes, if I lean back just right, I can see the profile of her face as she smiles. Usually, if something funny happens, the first thing I do is to look and see if she is smiling or even better see and hear her laugh. I love to see her smile. I love to hear her laugh. I think, every once in a while, she doesn't laugh enough.

We like to have little contests. One starts as soon as we finish supper and sit in our chairs. We don't have a name for it and the rules are simple: whoever has to get up and go to the potty first is the loser. I usually lose, but it's usually a pretty tight race between Beaux Bo and my sweetie. This week she is winning with three points, Beaux Bo has one point and I have zero. The reason the score may not add up to seven points is due to the rule that states if we decide to go at the same time, there are no losers. It would probably be best if you didn't tell her that you know about this contest. She would probably deny it or say that it was just another one of my stories.

I really don't watch as much TV as she thinks I do. A lot of the time I'll doze off for about half of the show, especially if it is something serious as compared to something funny. I just hope that she doesn't want to discuss the plot after the show is over. I'm pretty sure she's not aware of my little naps. Another thing I do, if the show's not holding my attention, is lean back and watch her face. When she smiles, I still see that twenty-something year old I fell in love with about a hundred years ago. I think back about all the things she has been through, a lot of really good stuff, and some not so good. All I can do as I sit there watching her is hope that I was with her every time she needed me, knowing there were probably times I wasn't.

Then we watch the news together, and by this time Beaux Bo has gone into the kitchen to clean out his food bowl, knowing that his Mama is going to wash and put the bowl up as soon as the news is over. We watch the news with some interest, occasionally mocking the news dude or gal, and wondering why in the world would they think we would need to know that. Then I come in here and do this, piddle on the computer, jot down some notes and thoughts and see what else has been going on in the world outside of our house as Beaux Bo curls up at my feet counting down to bedtime. I really don't know what all my best gal does, but I can hear her making those familiar housekeeping noises and, when things are quiet, I can hear her turning the pages as she reads one of her favorite magazines looking for new recipes or neat things to decorate our home.

Then, usually around midnight, my sweet Amber comes to the door and her sweet soft voice says, "Are you going to stay up all night messing with that dang computer, or are you coming to bed?"

With that said, we check the doors, turn on the alarm system, tell Beaux Bo one last time to go potty, take all our medications, brush our teeth, turn down the bed, slide between the fresh, sweet feeling sheets, go over our schedule for tomorrow, hug, kiss, say goodnight, sweet dreams and then, "I love you," as I reach and turn off the lamp.

THE END

A Gathering of Words
A Train of Thought

A series of heartwarming books based on a small-town fellow making his way in the world.

You'll want to read these stories out loud to someone — **They're that good!**

What people are saying:

"Reading *A Train of Thought* is like eating potato chips: You can't stop with one chapter, you gotta have more!"

"Love your book, Terry!"

"A legend is born!"

"I can't wait for your next book to come out — this is even better than I had imagined!"

"An easy read and quite entertaining."

"Terry, I've finished your great book. Congratulations on publishing such an entertaining volume."

Turn the page for an excerpt from
A Gathering of Words – A Train of Thought.

THE SECRET OF THE WASHITA AND ME

At twenty-five, I was foreman on a steel gang. A steel gang was a high priority gang with some of the most talented and specialized personnel in the engineering department. I was honored to be given the opportunity, especially at such a young age, and with less than a year's experience as a foreman.

We were working on the main line track between Davis and Dougherty, Oklahoma. This portion of track follows the Washita River as it cuts its way through the beautiful Arbuckle Mountains. The scenery was sometimes a distraction from the work at hand. About twenty to thirty feet from one side of the track were the steep walls of the Arbuckles and on the other side, within only a few feet, was the drop off into the Washita River. The river and track looked like a giant snake winding its way through the 350 foot granite walls that run for about fifteen miles through this area.

We were changing out the old rail, which has a tendency to wear out as trains 5000 - 7500 feet long traversed around the curves. The old rail was replaced with new strands of rail, each ¼ mile long, which weighed 119 pounds every three feet. We would begin work every morning at 6 a.m. and shut down by 2 p.m. in an effort to avoid the heat of the day.

After several weeks, we were finishing up with the last strand of rail and had plans to let the gang go early, in order to prepare for the move to the next work location. We had cleared the main track and were in the process of preparing the work equipment for moving, when the first train passed us moving southbound. Within several minutes of it having passed us we heard the train transmit on the radio, "Emergency, emergency, emergency! Our train has derailed!"

The train had derailed several hundred feet prior to the new rail we had just finished laying, but before the train came to a stop, several hundred feet of the freshly laid rail had been damaged. There were several hopper cars, once loaded with corn, derailed and leaning on their sides against the steep granite wall. Two of the cars had been ripped open and corn was covering the ground and track. It was necessary to walk through corn up to your waist to inspect the damage. It was determined that the derailment was caused by one of the hopper cars leaking out most of the corn on one side of the car, causing it to become unbalanced, so that as it entered the curve it leaned and its wheels left the rail, derailing the car.

After several hours, the train, the derailed cars and the corn were finally cleared so that we could begin making repairs to the track. It was terribly hot and humid as we worked well into the night, repairing the track and once again relaying the damaged rail. After finishing the repairs and opening the track for trains, the roadmaster felt it would be necessary for the track to be walked and inspected after each train through the remainder of the night. I volunteered for the job. I knew it was a tough job, but the pay was good.

After everyone left, I built a campfire not far from the track and waited for the first train. The first train rolled by slowly, after which I walked the track. I returned to the campfire and tried to get comfortable, because I knew from talking to the dispatcher earlier that it was going to be over an hour before the next train. As I sat there tired and miserably dirty, all I could think of was how great a cool refreshing shower would be. Then I became aware of the sounds of the river as it rolled by just fifty feet away. I began to think how nice it would be to wash a couple of layers of dirt and dried sweat off, not to mention the fact that it would recharge me and make the remainder of the night more tolerable. After all, I did have my suitcase in the truck with a nice clean change of clothes.

That's when I decided to disrobe and take a needed bath in the cool waters of the Washita River. I think I have pointed this out to some of you previously, but this is just another example of the fact that sometimes 'smart' and I don't get along. Anyway, I carefully climbed down the steep bank toward the rolling river. As I reached the water's edge, I sat my railroad lantern down on a nearby rock and looked into the water. I knew the water was moving with some force but figured I would just ease down into the water and hang onto the rocky bank.

As I eased down toward the water, the rock I was standing on dislodged and sent me tumbling into the river. Before I could react, I had washed fifty feet or so down river. I finally got upright and could feel the bottom with my feet, but the force of the water was more than I could handle as I continued my trip down river. The only chance I had was to try and get close enough to the bank to grab hold of something. Finally, I was able to grab hold of an old log that had become lodged into the bank. For the first time I was able to look back and try to spot my lantern--I couldn't see it. The bank was too steep for me to try to climb. I knew I didn't want to take a chance and go further down stream, so I began to work my way back upstream by holding on to rocks, logs and briers.

After about thirty minutes I could finally see the lantern -- It looked like it was a mile away. I began to get extremely tired and would periodically stop to find a location where I could wedge myself between boulders in order to rest my arms. Still, the bank was too steep to climb up so I continued upstream. Finally, I reached the lantern, but had to wait a few minutes because I was too weak to pull myself out of the water. Just as I pulled myself up on the bank, the next train slowly approached. I decided that my best bet was to lie between the rocks until the train passed. I didn't think I wanted to explain my nakedness to a bunch of talkative railroaders.

The train seemed to take forever to pass, but I was finally able to climb up to the track, walk a short distance to my truck, tend to the cuts and scrapes that I could reach, and at last put on a clean, dry set of clothes. I walked the track and made my inspection and returned to my smoldering campfire.

I sat down, leaned back and took a deep breath as I looked up to see the slight glow beginning to appear in the eastern sky behind the silhouette of the Arbuckle Mountains. Life felt good. This was an amazing night. I was a lucky man. As I sat there, I made the decision that it would be a long time before anyone would know about the events of that night.

Thirty-six years is probably long enough.

Did you enjoy Terry's stories? Would you like more?

Be watching for his next book in the A Gathering of Words series:

A Scattering of Memories

Coming Soon!

Want more Terry?

Keep up with him online at:

Facebook.com/TerryBeckWords

TerryBeckBlog.blogspot.com

Terry is also available for speaking engagements.
Please contact him at terry-beck@att.net.

Turn the page for a sneak peek at
A Gathering of Words – A Scattering of Memories

A Gathering of Words

A Scattering of Memories

by Terry Beck

ANTICIPATION

I woke to the smell of coffee. Man, I wish coffee tasted as good as it smells. I never opened my eyes. I just rolled over in the lower bunk, punched the pillow a couple of times, and tried to fall back to sleep. It would still be an hour or so before time for me to get up. As I lay there trying to convince myself that I was asleep, I heard Pop cough, clear his throat and turn on the radio. Then it hit me - I have a date tonight! I open my eyes and stare at the sagging springs of the bunk above me. No longer trying to go back to sleep, I start running through the things I'll need to get done before the date. The hard part was already over. I had finally gathered the courage to ask her out. Time had gotten away from me as I heard the sound of Pop's heavy work shoes on the hardwood floor of the hallway. I pulled my feet up from the foot of the bed as Pop reached down to shake my feet as always (something I always hated) and said "Time to get up TD, you're going to be late".

I quickly rolled out of bed, partly because I was anxious to get the day started, but mostly because in a one bathroom house with seven people it was best not to tarry. I sat with Pop at the kitchen table eating my cereal, listening to the deep morning voice on the radio as he let us know what was going on around town. Then Pop said, "You better get in there and brush your teeth and comb your hair. I'm fixin' to go wake up your mom and your brothers".

As I'm combing my hair, I hear my four younger brothers stirring in the bedroom. Then, as I stand at the lavatory trying to brush my teeth, the parade starts. It was as though I wasn't there as they brushed by me to use the bathroom. It wasn't unusual for my youngest brothers, eight or nine years my junior, to stand at the facility two at a time if they needed to go badly enough. I quickly finish up in the bathroom and go back in the bedroom to get dressed, passing Mom in the hallway as she's putting on her robe.

I pick out my newest pair of white Levi Jeans to wear, then, remembering my date, hang them back in the closet, saving them for the big date that night. Noticing the time, I quickly get dressed, thinking I needed to get to school a little early just in case I see her in the lunch room before class starts. I grab my school books and walk into the kitchen just as Pop is getting ready to leave for work. I lean down and kiss Mom on the cheek and say goodbye, and she asks if this was the day of the big date. As Pop walks by me, he looks down at my feet and says, "If you have a date tonight, you better make sure you shine them shoes", and walks out the door.

Driving to school, I begin thinking about my date again when it hit me. I had forgotten to ask Mom if I could use her car for the date. I hadn't wanted to ask her in front of Pop because he would have said there was nothing wrong with my car and there was no reason to use Mom's. Oh well, I'll get home before Pop and I'll ask her . If she says no, my old car cleans up pretty good. About that time I pull into the half full parking lot at school. As I walk up to the school building I turn and look back toward the parking lot to see if she's here yet. Nope, no sighting. Maybe she's already inside. I make my way into the building and stop by my locker to drop off my books, then stroll into the lunch room to the usual table.

There are already several of my buddies sitting there. Some laughing and talking and some racing to get homework finished. Everybody seems a little more energetic and excited about the day, even the teachers, because it's Friday. The guys start talking about their plans for the night - meeting at the Maid, maybe going to the dance, maybe playing some miniature golf...and the possibilities went on. Just for a moment I kind of wished I didn't have a date because Friday night with the guys is always fun. Then I look across the room as it begins to fill up. There she is, sitting with her friends at their usual spot. Man, she sure looks pretty, as all the thoughts of my buddies faded. Then the bell rings and it's time to go to home room.

Classes seemed to just crawl by. I saw her between classes from a distance a couple of times. She just didn't seem as excited about our date as I was. Then lunchtime finally arrived and the usual guys and I were eating lunch and talking about the weekend plans. When one of the self proclaimed "experienced" guys found out that I had a date, he felt that it was his duty to make a smart ass remark about my upcoming date and the girl I had the date with. I don't remember my exact response, but I can remember a feeling of anger and a need to protect the girl's honor. All I wanted was to have a good time, and not make a fool out of myself. My date wasn't any of his business anyway.

I did well in sports, in school politics, and my grades (well, they weren't bad for somebody that never studied), but for some reason girls scared me to death. Now, don't get me wrong; I had girls as friends and I actually had girlfriends, but girls just made me a nervous wreck. If the decisions were left to me, without any hints from the girl, I was totally confused about kissing and the proper timing thereof, and hand holding or putting my arm around her was mental torture. I always felt pressure to be someone that I wasn't.

The final bell eventually rang and the stampede to the parking lot was on. I had seen, and even waved at her a couple of times, but managed to go the whole day without saying a word to her. I just hoped that she hadn't forgotten our date. I rushed home and found Mom out in the backyard hanging clothes on the clothes line. I asked if I could please use her car for my date that night. She paused, then said she really didn't like being without her car. I told her she could use my car, plus I would wash her car and clean and vacuum the inside. She agreed as long as I would clean the tires as well. I backed her car out into the driveway and began vacuuming and cleaning the inside. I was going to have to hurry if I was going to get everything done in time.

As I was working on the car, one of my younger brothers walked up with a baseball and a couple of gloves and wanted to know if I'd play catch with him. I told him I really didn't have time, but if he would clean the tires while I cleaned the rest of the car, I would play catch with him for fifteen minutes after we got though. He agreed and we went about the business of cleaning the car. I didn't need to show my younger brother how to clean the tires because we had all worked at my Dad's body shop at one time or another, and when he finished painting a car it was always our job to clean the tires and wheels. Pop always said letting a freshly painted car leave with dirty tires is like going somewhere in a new suit and wearing old scuffed up shoes.

We finished the car, after Mom had pointed out a couple of spots that we had missed, and went out in the backyard to play catch. Before long the other three brothers and a couple of neighborhood kids had wandered up and we had a full-fledged game going. Forty-five minutes later I woke up to the fact that I still had things to do before the big date and now I was going to have to really rush. First I went to get gas in Mom's car. As soon as I got back, Mom said if I didn't have plenty of gas in my car, I needed to put some in it, so I was off to Mr. Dewbre's Store again.

I rushed home from the store and ran into the house to take a shower. It was my lucky day - the bathroom was vacant. I finished up my shower, and was standing at the mirror combing my hair when I noticed a huge pimple on my forehead. Of course I had to mash around on it which just made it look worse. I saw some of Mom's makeup, dabbed some on a finger and tried to cover up my blemish. I looked at it from several angles and decided that it now looked like a huge pimple with makeup on it. So, I wiped it off thinking, "Well maybe the huge pimple would distract her from noticing my huge ears, huge nose and freckles".

I was running late, so I quickly got dressed into my new white Levi jeans, my favorite shirt, socks and...crud! I hadn't shined my good shoes and what was worse, I couldn't find them. I let out a holler, "Has anybody seen my slip-on shoes?", as I walked into the kitchen thinking I was going to be late for sure. There sat Pop, putting a shine on my shoes. Man, what a break as I grabbed my shoes and headed back down the hall and Pop said that I could use some of his "smellum" if I wanted to. I put on some of his Old Spice, looked at myself in Mom's full length mirror for a final check...it would have to do, as I headed for the door. Mom yelled to be careful and Pop hollered for me not to be out late, and to come home as soon as I take her home. I hopped in the car and backed out of the driveway. (I don't think I ever told Pop thank you, or Mom either, for that matter.)

I had been so rushed I had forgotten about my nerves. As I got closer to her house I finally got a little nervous, but it was the good kind. The car looked sharp, I smelled good, and my shoes were shining. I pulled up in front of her house, got out of the car, and started walking to the front door. About halfway there I turned around and looked at the car. Yep, it looked good. As I continued the walk to the front door, I checked to make sure that my shirt tail was tucked in, then I checked to see if the front of my hair was okay with my hand and felt Hell's pimple on my forehead. Crud, I had forgotten about that! Oh well!

I knocked on the door and her mother invited me in. We made small talk for a few minutes and then she walked in. I couldn't believe that she was so pretty. Her mother said something, probably about having fun and being careful.

As we walked to the car, I couldn't believe I was so lucky…and man was she pretty.

And that's all I'm gonna say about the evening…

www.ingramcontent.com/pod-product-compliance
Lightning Source LLC
Chambersburg PA
CBHW070807100426
42742CB00012B/2285